Rail-trail Guide to California

Recreation Trails on Railroad Grades

P9-BID-727

Rail-trail Guide to California
Recreation Trails on Railroad Grades

Fred Wert

Infinity Press

Published by Infinity Press,
P.O. Box 17883, Seattle, WA 98107-1883.

Manufactured in the United States of America.

Edited and designed by Melissa Page
Maps by Fred Wert
Photographs by Fred Wert
Photographs pages 101 & 174, Tuolumne County Historical Society
Cover photographs by Fred Wert
Author photograph by Melissa Page
Cover design by Joan Schlicting

Library of Congress Cataloging-in-Publication data
Wert, Fred, 1949-
     Rail-trail Guide to California / Fred Wert
     p. cm.
ISBN 1-883195-02-2

Library of Congress Catalog Number 95-75832

PREFACE

California is a land of rapid change. Hidden amidst today's changing landscape is the abandonment of railroad tracks throughout the state. Many short segments and a few long segments of railroad track are no longer economical for commerce. However, this resource can be re-utilized for an entirely different type of transportation: non-motorized travel. A railroad grade becomes a rail-trail.

The tremendous volume of cars used for transportation in California has resulted in congestion and other negative impacts on communities. Alternate modes of transportation, such as light rail, bicycling, and walking are now being considered and given greater value in transportation planning. Rail-trails provide the greatest benefit for non-motorized travel due to their wide flat surfaces, gentle grades, and locations in densely populated areas.

Rail-trails are a public amenity. They provide recreational opportunities for many citizens who would otherwise have few safe alternatives. They also preserve a part of history in a land of change. By preserving railroad corridors for use as rail-trails, the public is also provided with potential corridors for still unknown future needs.

There is an urgency in creating rail-trails. Once a railroad abandons a line, the land can revert to many individual property owners making the grade nearly impossible to re-assemble. It is imperative that citizens and public officials together embrace the concept of creating rail-trails long before the rails are removed. Plans for non-motorized routes need to be part of comprehensive planning documents, transportation plans, recreation plans, and public improvement plans in general. People need to be prepared to create a trail when the rails are gone, and in many cases, before the tracks are removed. There are also several successful trails built in California alongside active railroads.

It is the goal of this book to increase public awareness of rail-trails, to help people experience the numerous benefits of rail-trails, and to encourage readers to help preserve more rail-trails. Rail-trails are a great public benefit, but it requires the public's participation in order for them to be created. Visit the rail-trails described in this book and get involved in your neighborhood to help preserve a wonderful legacy amidst the everchanging California.

Fred Wert, *Seattle, 1995*

ACKNOWLEDGMENTS

Just as it takes many people to build a rail-trail, it has taken the help of many people to write this book. Their support, interest, cooperation, and knowledge have been inspirational to me. I would like to thank:

Alan Williams, Andrew Oshita, Andy Anderson, Artemas Ginzton, Barbara Erwine, Ben Burto, Beth Bertke, Beth Chacon, Carlos Porrata, Craven Alcott, Dee Swanhouser, Dennis Mulgannon, Don Gilliland, Donna Mitzel, Easy, Fred Mailey, Gayle Likens, Gary Tate, Gretchen Stranzl-McCann, Jason Baker, Jim Eicher, Jimmie Lee, Joe Inch, Judy Muetz, Julie Fisher, Karen Suiker, Ken Wells, Lanny Waggoner, Mark Miller, Martin Matarrese, Michael Jackson, Mickey Karagan, Mike Matsuoka, Mike Parks, Pam Conners, Patricia Wagner, Paul Johnson, Pete Kolibaba, Rick Leflore, Ron Blakemore, Sandy Coambs, Sherri Miller, Stan Bales, Steve Gazzano, Steve Jantz, Steve Petterle, Terry Hanson, Tony Iacopi, Tony Perez, and Virginia Jones.

Special thanks to Charlie Willard for his review and suggestions, Joan Schlicting for the cover design which includes her own image, and Melissa Page for her assistance in researching the trails and outstanding job of editing and designing the book.

DISCLAIMER

Every effort has been made to insure that all of the facts presented in this book are correct. However, environmental and administrative changes may make some of the information obsolete. The author and publisher make no claims as to the safety of travel on these trails. Travel on these trails at your own risk. Please check with the trail manager before using any trail.

TABLE OF CONTENTS

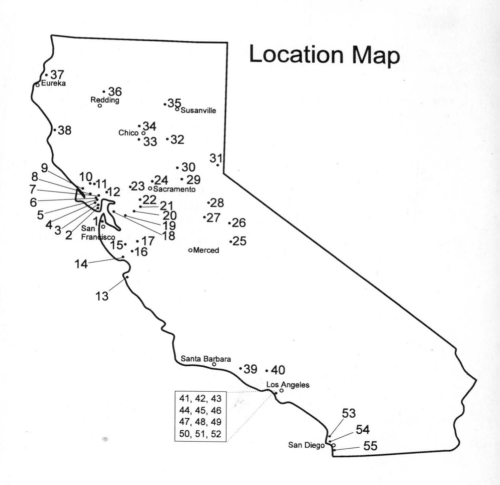

Location Map

INTRODUCTION

Railroads have been one of the most important transportation systems in the development of the United States. At the turn of the century, they were the most viable means of the long distance transport of goods and people over land. Ships and barges were very useful where there was water, but the midwest and west did not have sufficient waterways to create a complete system. Railroads provided a way to connect all parts of the United States and in those days carried tremendous loads at very high speeds for the times

At the peak of the railroads, there were more than 400,000 miles of main line track in the United States and many more miles of short line logging and mining railroads. With the increased development of the interstate highway system, trucks began to take over many of the tasks of hauling goods, especially for short distances. They had the advantage of being able to go anywhere there was a road and roads are less expensive to build than railroads. The increased availability of cars and commercial airlines decreased the demand for rail passenger service even more. The result is that by 1994, more than 160,000 miles of main line railroads had been abandoned throughout the United States.

Railroads will continue to abandon lines. Railroad companies are in direct competition for business with shipping, air freight, and trucks for hauling goods. It can be very expensive to maintain railroad lines especially if there is little "traffic" (railroad cars) shipped along the line. Floods, fires, rains, and earthquakes all impact the railroad lines. The standard gauge rails must be within tight tolerance to the standard 35 1/2" width or the trains come off the tracks. When the cost for maintenance is greater than the revenue being received from hauling cars, the railroad, as a private business, needs to seriously consider if it is in their best interest to continue operations. Many of the lines that have been abandoned lost traffic to trucks and were considered uneconomical by the railroads to continue operations.

RAIL-TRAILS

Rail-trails are trails built within the railroad corridors of either active or abandoned railroads. These trails convert the gentle grades and curves made by the railroad into outstanding shared-use corridors. The railroads often moved a great deal of earth, tunneled through mountains, or built tremendous bridges in order to pass smoothly through the rough contours of the land surface. When the railroads cease operations, they leave behind a continuous, narrow ribbon of land. Often, with a relatively small amount of effort from public or private sources, the abandoned corridor serves as a fine trail even without further improvements. With improvements, depending upon the surface, rail-trails are ideal for all types of non-motorized trail uses from baby buggies to bicycles, from in-line skating to cross-country skiing, from walkers to long distance runners.

Unique Features and Qualities of Rail-Trails

Rail-trails by their very nature offer many unique features and qualities. The roadbed left by the railroads, the long distances they travel, the connections between communities are all characteristic of rail-trails. These features allow rail-trails to significantly enhance city and regional trail systems. Rail-trails are valuable because:

They connect communities. In many places in the West railroads were the first long distance transportation system. Communities were built around the railroads with the distances between them dictated by how far a steam engine could travel before refueling and watering. The towns grew up with the railroad as the focal point. When the railroads cease operations, communities find an abandoned corridor ideal for a trail running through the middle of town, sometimes right down the main street. Their value now is not transporting goods but allowing citizens to travel in and through their communities without using motorized assistance.

They have an already established route. Determining the best route can be one of the more time and effort consuming tasks in the development of any new trail. In the mountains, route finding is concerned with grades, water crossings, soils, attractive features, views, avalanche exposure, and many additional aspects related to the natural terrain. In rural and urban areas issues include property ownership, buildings, roads, jurisdiction limits, land costs, and getting the support of residents. Rail-trails are built on grades which are already established, thus saving the trail proponents incredible amounts of work.

The trail is already built. Railroads moved a tremendous amount of earth, dug tunnels, and built numerous trestles in order to establish their gentle routes. The road beds were designed to support huge weights and for the local weather conditions. The abandoned railroad roadbeds, after the rails and ties are removed, provide an ideal base for a trail. In fact, in many places the only preparation necessary for conversion to a trail is to remove the rails and ties. Often these grades are built better and higher than the neighboring highways to withstand floods and, in some cases, the railroad grades have been used for evacuating people during flooding. In most places, especially in urban areas, it would be unfeasible to build such a road bed today, especially for trail purposes.

They have gentle grades.   The first engines were not very powerful and had trouble pulling heavy loads up steep grades. Speed and efficiency are very important for railroads and so railroad tracks were built with the minimum grades, usually never exceeding 2.2% for main lines. This means that a trail built on an old railroad grade is suitable for all types of uses (depending on the surface), from wheelchairs to in-line skating. Many trail users specifically search out rail-trails because they greatly appreciate the gentle grades.

They accommodate special-needs trail users. The gentle grades and generally wide, smooth surfaces offered by rail-trails are attractive to many people who have mobility limitations yet desire to get out and exercise. The elderly, physically challenged, those confined to wheelchairs, small children riding tricycles or their first bicycle, babies in baby-carriages or taking their first steps, dog sled teams, beginning cross-country skiers, horse drawn wagons, and other special-needs users all, in their own ways, appreciate the easy trail conditions.

They are accessible. "Accessible" nowadays usually refers to accessible by persons in wheelchairs and this sense certainly applies to rail-trails. Many rail-trails have been paved and are wide enough and have gentle enough grades to allow such access. But they are also accessible because they are often at lower elevations which are snow-free more of the year than the many mountain trails. In addition, rail-trails are often bisected by road crossings providing numerous places to get on or off the trail. This is a contrast to trails in mountains that often have only one trailhead.

They can provide funding for their development and management. Because railroad lines travel great distances, often through urban areas, and because they have a right-of-way usually wider than the grade, there is an opportunity to share the corridor with many types of utilities. Many agencies that manage rail-trails generate operating funds from the leasing of sub-surface and air rights for utilities such as power, water, sewer, phone, fiber optic cables, natural gas pipelines, and oil pipelines. The abandoned lines provide a very easy place to locate these utilities at a fraction of the cost of creating a new corridor, especially through a densely populated urban area.

They can serve as dikes. Many railroads were built near water courses or bodies of water because the railroads so valued flat or gentle grades. Most railroad companies built their lines so that they would not have to rebuild each year and, therefore, built them above the 100 year flood levels. The resulting grades now serve as potential dike structures and, when converted to trails, provide a safe haven during heavy flooding of the neighboring low-lying lands.

They preserve historic structures. Most railroads were built more than fifty years ago which qualifies them for historic status under many laws. Even the railroad grades themselves qualify, and some are on historic registers, recognizing the sometimes heroic measures taken in their construction. Along with the grades are trestles, tunnels, train depots, signal towers, and other artifacts, all of which have tremendously increased value when the railroad is converted to a trail. While these features may have been viewed as infrastructure while the railroads were running, they become accessible history when preserved as part of the rail-trail experience.

They provide economic opportunities. People who use rail-trails do so primarily for recreation. Outings may often include purchase of food, lodging or rental from the businesses near the rail-trails. The rail-trail concentrates recreation activities in a specific area, often generating sufficient business to sustain a new venture almost exclusively due to the trail use. The Lafayette-Moraga Trail is one which has been studied and shown to provide a positive economic benefit to the two communities for which it is named and through which it passes.

They preserve and enhance wildlife habitat. Most railroads acquired a fifty to one-hundred foot wide right-of-way and placed the tracks right down the middle. The actual graded section (the "grade") used for the tracks is usually no wider than fifteen feet. The area on both sides of the track was generally not used by railroads and allowed to grow naturally, often with native plant communities. As a result, there are locations where the only native flora for miles around is located next to the rail-trail. This area can include rare native plant species as well as cover for wildlife.

CREATING RAIL-TRAILS

While converting railroads to trails is in many ways easier than starting with nothing, the conversion process can be arduous. Understanding how railroads operate and the role of the Interstate Commerce Commission (ICC) in the development of rail-trails, will help improve chances for a successful conversion.

The ICC

At the turn of the century the United States government saw the development of railroads as the key to prosperity and the development of the west. They wanted to encourage railroads to build tracks everywhere rather than competing directly against each other for the most profitable routes. In order to expand the railroad miles, the federal government provided many concessions and often deeded federal land to the railroads. This often created a situation where a railroad that served a shipper had, in effect, a monopoly on that shipper for rail service. It was unlikely and often impractical (without concessions) for another railroad to build a siding directly to the same shipper to try and attract their business. Therefore it was conceivable that a railroad could just keep raising rates without any real choice for the shipper. As a protection, the Interstate Commerce Commission (ICC) was entrusted with regulating tariffs (prices charged) for railroads dealing with interstate commerce.

An even greater risk existed for shippers who built businesses next to the railroad to ship and receive goods; the railroad might simply choose to stop operating. This could easily put the shipper out of business, especially in the days before trucking was an alternative. Even today, some very heavy produce such as coal is not economical to haul long distances by truck. Again, the government stepped in and created regulations to prevent railroads from having the ability to arbitrarily abandon shippers.

Under ICC regulations, when a railroad would like to cease operations of a line, it must first apply through a legal regulatory process before the ICC to obtain permission to cease operations. This process is called abandonment. This is done for the protection of shippers along the line. The railroad presents its case for why it would like to abandon service, usually demonstrating an economic loss to the company for continuing service. There is an opportunity for shippers, and any other party, to comment on this request and sometimes the comments are numerous and loud. If the ICC Commissioners feel that the railroad is being unfairly required to lose money for the benefit of other businesses, the ICC usually allows abandonment. Once the ICC has issued an abandonment notice, the railroad is no longer required to provide service, can take up the rails and ties, and can dispose of the land. (Note: As this book goes to press it appears that Congress may dissolve the ICC and move its abandonment overview authority to the Department of Transportation.)

Railroad right-of-way ownership

An important part of any rail-trail project is getting control of the railroad right-of-way once the railroad abandons so that it can be used by the public as a trail. Unfortunately, this is not always a very straight-forward transaction. As long as the railroad was operating, few people had an interest in investigating the ownership of the land over which the railroad operated. The land appeared to be under the possession and therefore ownership of the railroad. When the railroad ceases operation, many people, usually adjacent property owners, become interested in the quality and type of title held by the railroad.

One of the common incorrect assumptions made by people who live adjacent to a railroad property which is abandoned is that the portion of the railroad right-of-way which abuts their land belongs to them. This very often is not the case at all, yet it is widely professed by those against public trails. The legal ownership is often so murky that most title insurance companies will not sell title insurance that covers railroad right-of-way property.

Why is it so difficult to determine just who owns the land? One of the problems involves finding the documentation pertaining to ownership. Of course, the original deeds or easements were valuable to the railroads and they were usually preserved by the railroad. But interpretation of the "quality" of title is sometimes open to debate. "Quality" of title refers to the likelihood that a court will agree with the apparent ownership. During the ensuing 100 years or so since the original sale, ownership and rights often become obscured.

Ownership might revert to the adjacent landowners. However, many of these adjacent parcels may have been re-sold several times since the original sale. If each of the deeds did not include the railroad property in the property description, there could be a gap in the chain of title and uncertainty as to whether the current adjacent property owner actually has any rights to the railroad grade at all. One method of clearing title is to file for "quiet title" action in the courts. This action basically allows an individual to make a public notice of a claim upon a parcel of land. If no one else can come forward and show proof of title, the title is "cleaned up" by the court. This process has backfired for people adjacent to abandoned railroad lines trying to get good title to the property when heirs to the original land owners came forward and took title.

Sometimes, adjacent landowners clearly have no legal claim to the railroad right-of-way. Many of the main line railroads in the west were built starting in the 1890's. One way that the railroads obtained land was through land grants from the federal government. If a railroad obtained the land through this method, then when they "abandon" the land with ICC permission, the land goes back to the federal government. If the federal government does not take possession of the land, only then does it pass to the current adjacent property owner.

Even when the railroad right-of-way appears to revert to the adjacent landowner, there is question as to when that reversion takes place. During the formation of the railroads, land was purchased from adjacent owners either as an easement or a deed with language referring to purchase "for railroad purposes". The courts have generally decided that these documents are not transfers of "fee" title, in which case all rights would transfer to the railroad with no reversionary interest on the part of the seller. However, since 1986, the courts have allowed that the railroad may be using the right-of-way "for railroad purposes" even after the rails and ties have been removed and it is in the interest of the government to keep the right-of-way intact for potential future operations. The method devised to make this possible is called railbanking.

Rail-banking

The rapid disappearance of a large number of railroad lines throughout the United States is a source of concern for many groups. The military has always viewed the railroads as a critical means of transporting personnel and equipment around the United States to protect our borders. At one time they even considered a plan to have inter-continental ballistic missiles mounted on railroad cars and constantly moving around the United States making them difficult targets to hit. The Commerce Department is concerned that a part of the infrastructure that has made the United States so competitive internationally is being destroyed. Those interested in energy conservation mourn the loss of the railroads for two closely related reasons. First, trains transport heavy materials long distances much more efficiently than alternative transportation methods. Second, using railroads for passenger service uses much less energy than the equivalent car traffic. Those interested in the railroads for shipping or passenger service lament the loss of routes that may be impossible to reclaim when economic or environmental issues make it desirable or perhaps even necessary.

As a result of all these concerns, a method of preservation of the railroad corridors was examined and adopted. In 1983, the National Trails System Act was passed, section 8 (d) of which held a provision called "railbanking." Railbanking attempts to preserve the most precious part of the railroads, the long continuous tracts of roadbed assembled many years ago and which would be almost impossible to assemble today. Railbanking allows the transfer of the railroad corridor intact from the railroad to the purchaser, provided the grade is not destroyed and the ICC retains control of future use of the corridor for railroad purposes.

A party may come forward within 30 days of the time an abandonment request is filed with the ICC and make a railbanking request, an expression of interest in purchasing the railroad corridor and keeping it intact should the railroad be given permission to abandon. This written request goes on file. When the railroad does file for abandonment, the ICC proceeds according to regulations. First, the ICC takes care of all issues related to the abandonment. Then they entertain requests by other railroads to purchase the line, even for short line (in-state) use. When all of these considerations have been addressed, they then look to see if any party has made a railbanking request. If so, they will ask the railroad if it is interested in participating in railbanking. If the railroad agrees, they will then allow a period of time for the railroad to negotiate a sale of their property rights to the railbanking requester.

Under normal abandonments which are not railbanked, "non-fee ownership" (a legal term for a type of ownership) passes to those parties who own the property interests. They are free to develop the railroad grade as they choose. Under railbanking this is not true. When the ICC has received confirmation from the railroad that they have sold their interests to the railbanking party, the ICC issues a Certificate of Interim Trail Use to the railbanking party. This certificate basically says that the ICC allows that party to use the land for trail purposes until such time as a bona fide railroad approaches the ICC and asks to purchase that land. At that time, the railbanking group must sell their ownership to the new railroad company. The key part of this process is that the ICC does not actually issue an abandonment approval to the railroad. Instead they issue a Notice of Interim Trail Use which relieves the railroad from providing service and allows them to salvage the line. This means that that land is still being used, or perhaps more accurately preserved, "for railroad purposes" which keeps intact the easements which were purchased for railroad purposes. No development which would interfere with a possible future railroad may take place on the railroad grade.

The practical outcome of this law is that a group or public agency can acquire a railroad's ownership interest in a railroad and the rails and ties can be removed. All the previous ownership rights of the railroad are passed onto the new, interim owner. Reversionary clauses in easements are not triggered. This law has been tested and upheld by the Supreme Court. It is a critical law in making conversions from railroads to trails possible. Without this law, the question of ownership is completely open. Many competing claims will be made for every potential parcel along the entire length of line. It is often difficult for even the courts to settle competing claims because many of the original documents are missing or ambiguous. In urban areas especially, failure to railbank a line can mean an agency has to negotiate or purchase rights from up to 200 individual owners per mile of railroad grade in order to clear title.

There is an extreme difference between allowing a railroad to go through a normal abandonment process through the ICC and obtaining a railbanking agreement. Many rail-trail proposals that do not include the benefits of railbanking have been quickly dismissed when agencies are faced with the daunting task of assembling many small parcels of land created by an abandonment. It is clear from past experience that railbanking is almost always a very critical step in the conversion of any railroad corridor to a trail.

Rail-Trail Development

A rail-trail is a valuable asset to a community. Visit communities that have rail-trails and you will find many people that use them, sometimes daily. They are generally held in high esteem by the parks staff, public officials, and especially trail users. It is often because its developers recognized the eventual benefits of a rail-trail that they succeeded in completing the daunting task of rail-trail development.

The development of a rail-trail can be a major undertaking. There are several factors which are critical in making a rail-trail a success.

1) Make people aware of the opportunity.

2) Organize a strong citizens' group that will continue to be operational beyond trail construction.

3) Identify a lead agency.

4) Get potential projects identified on government planning documents so they qualify for most funding.

5) Find adequate funding.

6) Understand and apply for railbanking when the railroad applies for abandonment.

7) Enlist public officials who are willing to understand railbanking, spend money, and take heat.

8) Include adjacent land owners and adjacent tenants in the process.

The most important aspect of rail-trail development is public awareness of the benefits of rail-trails. Rail-trail developers must have a clear vision of what they want to accomplish and the ability to be tenacious in the face of opponents. They need to be flexible in order to overcome obstacles encountered during development. Only by being vocal and persistent can they hope to sway public officials who might otherwise side with rail-trail opponents when controversy arises, even when it can be shown that rail-trails serve the greatest public good.

The development of rail-trails has escalated in the last ten years as many more railroad lines have been abandoned. Nationally there are now more than 700 completed rail-trails with more than 1,000 additional trails being planned. They have been built in almost every state and total more than 7,000 miles. When you discover opposition to your local project, take heart; there have been many prior obstacles overcome and there are many success stories to share.

With solid citizen support, almost any rail-trail project can succeed in one way or another. But the single action that will, if possible to take, save proponents the most time and effort is railbanking. This means that plans must begin even before a railroad grade is abandoned. Identify an organization or agency willing and capable of purchasing the grade. A letter of railbanking intent must be submitted to and kept on file by the ICC. Federal, state, and local public agencies as well as private, non-profit groups such as The Trust for Public Land, have purchased grades in the past. Consider approaching such a group early. A railbanking letter commits no one to completing a rail-trail project, but only with a such a letter on file can the railbanking process begin once a railroad abandons. Successful railbanking eliminates the need for lengthy negotiations or quiet title action on each and every parcel along the corridor and, therefore, greatly decreases the work involved and increases the chances of success.

At the national level, the Rails-to-Trails Conservancy (RTC), located in Washington D.C., is an an advocate organization specifically focused on rail-trails. RTC works with federal agencies, promotes rail-trails within the recreation community, and provides encouragement and resource materials to local groups working on rail-trails.

Funding

Rail-trails have a great head start on many other public trail projects in that the route and trail sub-grade are already in place. In some cases the costs to make the trail usable may be minimal. In other situations the costs can be comparable to road construction. For example, in an urban environment the movement of utilities may be required. In a rural setting, trestles may need to be rebuilt or replaced. In any location, a trail developed without the benefits of railbanking will require the purchase of numerous parcels of land, often in private ownership. Still, funding can come from any number of sources, from volunteer labor to transportation funding grants. The opportunities for funding are as numerous as the imagination of the trail proponents. Some options include:

ISTEA. ISTEA stands for the Intermodal Surface Transportation Efficiency Act which is revamping the process for distribution of federal dollars for transportation. In the past, the emphasis was on building roads and the interstate highway system. The interstate system is now largely complete and the interest has shifted to funding other transportation systems. This innovative program allows transportation dollars to be spent on all types of transportation projects, not just roads. Rail-trails, bike paths, bike plans, and greenways all qualify for funding. The program is administered at the state level and it is critical for groups interested in rail-trails to make sure that the state project selection criteria encourage non-motorized projects. ISTEA has so much money available it dwarfs all other sources of rail-trail funding so it is well worth the effort to pursue. This funding source requires reauthorization in order to provide continued funding for rail-trail projects.

State and local transportation funds. In a number of areas a portion of the gas tax or other transportation taxes are being set aside for non-motorized use. Call your local public works department and inquire about dedicated funds. Learn about these sources and get applications prepared well in advance of deadlines.

Recreation funds. There are some recreation-specific funds available for parks and outdoor recreation facilities. While rail-trails may qualify, you will have to be creative in order to compete against other more traditional projects such as ball-fields. Ask your local or state parks directors for information about these funding sources.

Utility projects. If you can get a utility company to lease part of the right-of-way, you have created an income stream to help build and maintain the rail-trail. With a long-term lease agreement providing a steady source of income, you can sometimes get an agency to borrow the development funding today and pay back the loan in the future. Approach your local utility company if this appears to be an option for your trail.

Grants from private foundations. User groups can obtain funding from non-governmental sources that can be used for many aspects of rail-trail development including planning, lobbying elected officials for money, and soliciting more contributions from the public. This approach can also be successful on small projects that do not take a great deal of funding.

Free labor. The Army National Guard, Boy Scout Troops, civic groups, and schools are all sources of free labor. These types of groups are always looking for "public service" projects. Your task is to find something attractive for them to do that is manageable. For example, the Corps of Engineers has designed bridges and trained bulldozer drivers by clearing rail-trail grades.

Mitigation. Many dams are in the process of being re-licensed by the Federal Energy Regulatory Commission. Part of this re-licensing process is to provide some type of local mitigation for the impact of the dam project on the environment. You can propose that they spend money to build your rail-trail project.

Contributions. Many companies will contribute materials or supplies to a project, especially if their owner or employees feel that it is for a good cause. Make the project visible before you approach them so that they know they will be publicly acknowledged for their contributions. Include them in walks along the proposed route so that they see what you are talking about.

Elected Representatives. Take your local, state, and federal elected representatives on walks along a rail-trail corridor. This is particularly effective if it is on a rail-trail where a federal agency is in the lead. All the managers of the agency will want to be there to meet the member of congress and of course they will have to support your project even more, especially if they obtain additional funding for your project.

These are just a few suggestions. The list is really as long as your imagination. Remember, the rail-trail will provide a positive public benefit for your community. Make as much of your community part of the project as you can from the start and the chances for successful completion will improve enormously.

Trail design

While all rail-trails share some similarities because they are on old railroad lines, there is a significant variation in the types of design between rail-trails. Some rail-trails are built on old logging railroad grades deep in the forests. These are often no more than narrow dirt paths with crude creek and river crossings. Some rail-trails are open that have had almost no improvements since the line was abandoned. At the other extreme are urban trails built to AASHTO (American Association of Highway Transportation Officials) guidelines: 10-12 feet in width, asphalt surfaces, signs, lighting, benches, gates, parking lots, toilets — everything the urban user has come to expect.

The important part of the design process is to include the public. They will tell you what they want. Visit other rail-trails and talk to the managers and the users. They will tell you what works and what doesn't work. Take the best ideas back to your project. Work incrementally.

RAIL-TRAILS IN CALIFORNIA

Railroad History

Railroads were an important part in the settlement and development of California. They were built for many different purposes. In some places they were built deep into the woods for the purpose of hauling logs out to the mills. In other places they were built high into the mountains to haul ore from mines back to refiners. In some urban areas electric lines were built specifically to move passengers. In several locations scenic railroads were built solely to transport passengers to viewpoints. However, the main line railroads were built to transport goods and passengers across the state, both north/south and east/west.

In general, few major long distance lines (although many short segments) have been abandoned in California -- only 837 miles of ICC controlled common carrier lines between 1977 and 1989. Appendix 3 contains a list of the most recent abandonments. Note that some of the lines that have been abandoned have been purchased for short-line operations and are still in use.

Abandonments

Every indication is that additional abandonments will occur, primarily on short segments or dead end lines. But there are still some potential long distance abandonments such as Willits to Eureka. It is important for rail-trail advocates to keep abreast of the changing economic plights of railroads as well as the shipper volumes. The closing of a single lumber mill served by a railroad can signal the impending abandonment of that line. You can keep up with the status of railroads by contacting the CALTRANS railroad office at 916-322-7750 and ask which lines are low volume and which are listed as Category 1 status in the railroads system diagram maps. Category 1 status is a term that means that the railroad intends to abandon the line within three years.

Rails with trails

The increasing congestion of cars and trucks on highways has renewed interest in rail passenger service. "Light rail" is seen by some as an opportunity to relieve this congestion. Naturally, light rail advocates view abandoned lines, or those up for abandonment, as ideal routes. In fact, preserving an abandoned line for just such a future use was the basis for the railbanking law. However, rather than displacing existing rail-trails, or choosing just one use, there is the viable option of having both light rail and a trail share the same right-of-way.

Railroad rights-of-way often are between 50 and 100 feet in width. The light rail systems are almost always single track and need only about 20 feet of right-of-way. This leaves ample space for a trail. The primary concern of the light rail operators is the liability for injury of trail users. This concern can usually be assuaged by including a suitable fence between the tracks and the trail users. In fact, the development of the trail may actually make the light rail corridor safer as it is unlikely a fence would be built alongside the light rail system if a trail did not exist.

There are already many examples of rails with trails, some in California. In some cases there is no fencing or other barrier at all. On the Alton Bikeway the separation is a thick shrub. On the Santa Fe Greenway in Richmond (north of Berkeley) the rail-trail is either on top of or underneath the elevated BART tracks. The AT&SF Trail in Irvine parallels the main line high-speed line separated by a utility corridor. In other locations a simple swale filled with water or blackberry bushes is sufficient to keep trail users off the tracks. In general, trail users stay on the trail.

Rail-trails and light rail can work together. The trail can be an access road to repair the light rail structures. Light rail passengers can use the trail to get to stations. Remember, all light rail users must walk to get to the trains, even if it's only from their car to the train. Sharing the right-of-way might help spread the value and cost of acquiring the land rather than only using 1/5 of the land acquired for light rail. Landscaping the trail is a value to the rail passengers. Seeing the light rail cars go past may be a not so subtle hint to the trail users to take the light rail. The trail users can use the light rail to make one way trips on the trail and return quickly to their starting point without retracing their steps. Rail-trail advocates should approach this opportunity as a win-win situation for both groups in order to achieve success. Remember, too, there may be a large overlap between the two user groups.

Rail-trails as part of trail systems

California has underway a number of long distance trail system projects. These include the Coastal Trail, the Bay Area Trail, The Bay Area Ridge Trail, the Cross Marin Bike Path, and the Sacramento to South Lake Tahoe Trail. This is a pattern similar to other states which have launched ambitious long distance trail projects. Rail-trails can sometimes be the primary ingredient in such a trail system. More likely in California, rail-trails provide short links that may otherwise be difficult to build. Because the railroads were built before most other development, the rights-of-way are often the only continuous, unobstructed property ownership through developed areas.

Potential Future Rail-trails

While the system of rail-trails in California is growing, the potential is even greater for the future. The precendents have been set. As more and more agencies and individuals recognize the strong public value of rail-trails, more projects will be completed. As more lines are abandoned or converted to light rail, more opportunities will be created.

This book is primarily a guide to the existing rail-trails. But it is also designed to ignite readers' curiosity about the potential for rail-trails in their own neighborhood, or anywhere they travel. In Appendix 2 is a list of rail-trails that are currently being discussed, planned, or are under construction. As part of every description of an existing rail-trail, I have tried to point out opportunities for expansion of that trail and links between it and other trails.

An even broader look is to consider all the possibilities regardless of current railroad operations. No one 15 years ago would have considered that many of the Chicago Milwaukee and St. Paul Railroad lines would become rail-trails. Then the railroad went bankrupt. It is important to be prepared for this potential for all lines in California, even the main lines. A major bankruptcy may make some lines uneconomical. A major earthquake could make a line too expensive to rebuild. Floods have washed out bridges which are very expensive to replace. Appendix 2 contains some ideas for potential rail-trails throughout the state that need further study, inclusion in agency planning documents, and trail champions. It is my hope that through your enjoyment of many of the rail-trails listed in this book you will take on the challenge of making these potential rail-trails a reality in the future.

USING RAIL-TRAILS

Rail-trails are great because they provide a wonderful arena for a great variety of recreational and transportation uses. Their gentle grades, good access, and generally wide surfaces are attractive to many users who would not consider traveling on a steep, narrow, mountain trail. The type of trail users include:

Walkers
People walking to work or to shop
Parents with children in strollers
People using manual or electric wheelchairs
People who can only walk on smooth, gentle surfaces
Children on tricycles or bicycles
Joggers/Runners
Race walkers
Bicycle commuters
Mountain bicyclists
Road cyclists
In-line skaters
Hikers
Cross-country skiers
People on horseback
People driving teams of horses
Dog sled teams

All these user groups make rail-trails popular, but they can also misuse trails they share with others. In order to retain the popular benefits of rail-trails, it is important for **all** trail users to cooperate with each other to enjoy and share the trail.

Trail Use Etiquette

There are some general rules that apply to all trail users.

1) Obey rules or regulations posted by the managing agency.

2) Stay on the trail. Going off the trail can harm the vegetation and alarm wildlife. It is also possible that you will be going outside the public right-of-way. Passing onto private property only decreases the chances of more rail-trails being built.

3) Keep to the right of the trail surface. Trail users can travel at different speeds. By keeping to the right there is an increased chance that the traffic will flow in a more enjoyable manner.

4) Let other trail users know that you are passing. If you are going faster than another user, let them know you are passing by using a bell or voice ("passing on your left") so they are not startled. This will make the trail experience more enjoyable for everyone.

5) Be courteous to all trail users. People using the trail are generally there for their own enjoyment. You want to have a good time and so do they. You are all on the trail rather than on some road so that you can have a good time.

6) Leave the trail in better shape than when you found it. Pick up litter, clear brush, particpate in clean up projects.

7) Report trail damage to the trail manager.

8) Leave all gates as you found them. This is an unwritten law in the rural areas where gates are important for keeping livestock under control. Urbanites need to understand how important this is to those who live adjacent to the trail.

Walkers/Hikers/Joggers

Walking is one of the most popular forms of outdoor recreation in the United States and especially in California where the weather is so mild. Rail-trails make a great place for everyone to walk, no matter what their abilities. However, just because walking is so basic and is such a simple activity, walkers still have responsibilities as trail users. The following are some things to consider as you walk along the rail-trail.

1) Try not to block the trail. One of the great luxuries of a rail-trail is that people can walk side by side and talk and look at each other, even hold hands. However, if the trail is crowded or other trail users are frequently passing you, walking side by side can be something of a moving blockade. Be aware of approaching trail users and share the trail. Allow ample room to pass even if the trail is not crowded. Remember that other trail users may be approaching and need to pass you from behind.

2) Keep pets leashed and close by. Many people enjoy the company of pets and take them on walks on a regular basis. Keep in mind though that they can be lethal threats to bicyclists or in-line skaters who are traveling at a greater speed. Pets can easily and unpredictably move across the trail surface and are not aware of the needs of other trail users as their owners must be.

3) Do not cut the trail. In the mountains cutting switchbacks is a major problem. Rail-trails normally do not have switchbacks but people on foot may try to get to the trail without using public access. Again, this may damage vegetation or wildlife habitat or good relations with adjacent landowners. Please use only public access points and do not cross through private land.

Bicyclists

Rail-trails are great for bicyclists. The gentle surfaces make peddling easy and fast. The gentle curves let the cyclist continue without braking to slow down. However, bicyclists need to take special precautions in order to share the trail with other users.

1) Always wear a helmet. The ease of going fast is countered by the potential serious damage if you should stop suddenly and impact the ground with your body. Studies show that a high percentage of bicycle accidents involve head injuries. Many people die by hitting their head on the ground, on an object, or with another person.

2) When overtaking other trail users let them know. Use a bell or voice ("on your left") so that they know you are coming. Make sure you know the way is clear in both directions before you pass. Even with a clearly spoken "on your left," someone mistakenly may move to the left. Bicycles move very quietly and they approach very quickly. If you surprise someone it is more likely to hurt you than them.

3) Be cautious around horses. Slow down, talk to the rider, make human noises, and be prepared to stop. Some horses never figure out that bicycles have humans on them. If unsure, just ask the rider what they would like you to do. You will certainly earn their respect. You will always lose in a pushing or kicking match with a frightened horse.

4) Be prepared. Keep your bicycle in good repair so that it does not break down. Carry a small tool kit and learn how to use it for yourself or to help another trail user.

5) Use lights at night. Rail-trails are supposed to be safer than roads, however, they are often much darker. The use of adequate lights, both front and rear, is paramount to safe night riding.

Equestrians

Rail-trails are popular with equestrians for many reasons. If conditions allow, they can ride side by side, they can see down the trail, they can ride fast if they choose, they can even hitch their horses to wagons. In Washington State, each year the John Wayne Pioneer Wagon and Riders Association leads a trip more than two hundred miles on a rail-trail. In rural and urban areas they can be one of the few places where they can travel for miles. However, rail-trails are generally open to all types of non-motorized use and equestrians need to adjust their riding style accordingly.

1) Use separate equestrian trails where provided. Some rail-trails have separate gravel or dirt paths adjacent to the main trail designed for equestrian use. Use these to help reduce encounters with other rail-trail users.

2) Stay on the trail. Horses can go many places that humans would not want to tread. But equestrians should not take advantage of this ability as their actions can create a great deal of damage to the rail-trail environment.

3) Know your horse. Only ride horses that will tolerate other people, likely encounters with fast cyclists, or unusual situations such as bridges or tunnels.

4) Walk or trot. You may have good control of your horse but you can surely scare those who do not know horses. This is a public trail, not a race course.

5) Announce your intentions. Let trail users know what you plan to do, then ask them for assistance if you need it. Not all trail users will like horses or know how to act around them.

Skaters

Another user group pleased with rail-trails is those who roller skate or use in-line skates. They have the ability to travel fast, but need a smooth surface. Most skaters are not comfortable using streets and rail-trails provide one of the best places to go. However, skaters should keep several things in mind.

1) Be cautious when passing people coming towards you or when you pass from behind. You know that you will not hit them with your arms or legs, but they do not necessarily know that. Ease up for a second, stand up, make it clear that you are paying attention to them and will change your stride to avoid them.

2) When skating in groups do not pass other skaters when other users are in the trail. The passing can look like you are taking up the entire rail-trail.

3) Announce that you are going to pass. This is particularly important when passing equestrians. It can also be critical for bicyclists who may never consider that a skater could go as fast as they do.

Special users

Rail-trails are also popular with a variety of special users.

1) Wheelchair users find rail-trails with hard surfaces one of the few recreational locations where they are not isolated. Whether self-propelled or using electric support, wheelchair users can go great distances on the gentle grades. People who race wheelchairs find the trails ideal training ground.

2) Those with physical challenges. This includes the elderly who do not have super strong legs, those on crutches recuperating from injuries, those with diseases such as cerebral palsy, or those with other motor development restrictions.

3) Race walkers simply love the smooth surface which is critical for their difficult stride.

4) Runners love a place to run without interruption and an out-and-back route where they can easily measure their distance and time.

5) Cross-country skiers enjoy the gentle grades and smooth surfaces. Rail-trails are ideal for beginners who do not need the challenge of steep grades. They are wide enough to allow both traditional tracks and skating tracks to be set side by side.

6) Sled dog mushers find a route which is long, wide and with good site distances for potential problems.

USING THIS BOOK

This book is a general reference guide to the rail-trails in California. At the beginning of this book is a map of California showing the location of each rail-trail listed in the table of contents. The trail descriptions are grouped by Northern California and Southern California. The Northern California and Southern California sections have short introductions. Within each trail section you will find some basic information about the trail, a description of what you will find, a map showing the trail route, and a photograph. The descriptions of each trail are organized as follows:

Trail Name: Each trail description includes the official rail-trail name. For those with no formal name, a name that generally describes the trail location has been assigned.

Endpoints: The endpoints are city names or street names in most cases. Because many of these rail-trails are likely to be extended by the managing agency, the actual end of the trail may be further than indicated in this book.

Length: The length is indicated in miles for a one-way trip. The elevation gain or loss is not generally included because it is usually not significant. Steep trails are noted in the trail descriptions with estimates of the percent grade. Main line railroads usually stayed below 2.2% grade. Some of the scenic and logging railroads approached 5% grades.

Surface: The surface is listed as asphalt, concrete, hard packed gravel, unimproved ballast, dirt, or some combination. Sometimes there will be both a paved and parallel soft-surface portion to a trail. A notification of "unimproved ballast" is an indication that there has been very little improvement of the surface and that it may be difficult for walking or riding a bicycle until it is improved. Some trails that are listed as gravel actually have solid rock as part of the surface, such as the Merced River Trail and the Old Railroad Grade up Mt. Tamalpias which will not be suitable for bicycles with narrow tires. In addition, some of the rocky sections may be hard on horses hooves. Check with the trail manager for a more detailed description of the surface.

Original Railroad: Where known, the original railroad name is listed along with the year the railroad began service. In some cases the year that it was abandoned and the year a trail was opened are also given.

Restrictions: Almost all of the trails listed in this book do not allow any type of motorized vehicles (motorized wheel chairs excepted), except for a few portions of a few trails. We will use the abbreviation "NMV" (no motorized vehicles) to designate this restriction. Any other significant restrictions based upon type of use are listed here.

Location: Listed is the closest city and county in which the rail-trail is located.

Trail Manager: Included for each trail is the organization that is responsible for managing the trail. It is advisable to call or write the trail managers to get the most up-to-date information since the surface conditions, use restrictions, and degree of development of these trails are subject to change. This is particularly true for rail-trails in rural or mountainous areas. A listing of the names, addresses, and phone numbers for each of these agencies is listed in Appendix 1.

Directions: In most cases the directions start from an interstate highway or a small community near the trail. These directions are to either the most popular trailhead or the one with the most parking. If appropriate, there is information on how to get to both ends of the trail and other good access points.

Description: There is considerable variation in the physical condition and the ambiance of these trails, from the concrete sidewalk of the Fairfield Linear Park to the wild, rugged natural terrain of the Merced River Trail. The description attempts to paint a picture of each trail and what you will see along the way. Connections at both ends, intersections with other trails, and possible future trail links are noted here.

Map: A map is included with each trail description showing the entire route. This map shows trailheads, access points, and points of interest. For additional maps, call the trail manager listed at the top of each description (see Appendix 1 for addresses and phone numbers). Note: since many of these rail-trails are new, many do not show up on regular maps or show up as railroads.

Photograph: A photo of each trail is included. For short trails this may capture the local atmosphere. Some longer trails would require a photo album to reveal their many aspects. A single photo can only give you a clue of what you will find when you visit.

The legend for all the maps is shown below:

LEGEND

Rail-trail	▬▬▬▬▬▬
Planned rail-trail	░░░░░░░░░░
Road/street	——————
Railroad Tracks	┼┼┼┼┼┼┼┼┼┼┼┼
Rivers, creeks	~~~~~~
Bodies of water	⬭
Trailhead	Ⓣ
North	▲ N
Boundaries	▱
Tunnel	⌣ ⌣
Parking	🅿
Mountain Peaks	△
Mileage Scale	0 Miles 1

1. Lands End Trail
2. Old Railroad Grade
3. Mill Valley-Sausalito Path
4. Larkspur Path
5. East West Trail Link
6. Levee Trail
7. Tiburon Lineal Park
8. Sir Francis Drake Bikeway
9. Tomales Bay Rail-trail
10. West County Trail
11. Joe Rodota Trail
12. Sonoma Bike Path
13. Monterey Bay Coastal Trail
14. Loma Prieta Grade
15. Bol Park Bike Path
16. Los Gatos Creek Trail
17. Creek Trail
18. Santa Fe Greenway
19. Shepard Canyon Bike Trail

20. Lafayette/Moraga Trail
21. San Ramon Valley Iron Horse Trail
22. Black Diamond Mine Trail
23. Fairfield Linear Park
24. Sacramento Northern Bike Trail
25. Merced River Trail
26. West Side Rails
27. West Side Railroad Grade
28. Sugarpine Railway Trail
29. El Dorado County Trail
30. Western States Pioneer Express Trail
31. Truckee River Bike Trail
32. Paradise Memorial Trailway
33. Midway Bike Path
34. Chico Airport Bike Path
35. Bizz Johnson Trail
36. Sacramento River Trail
37. Hammond Trail
38. MacKerricher State Park

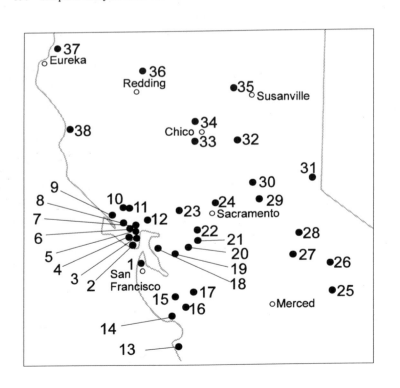

NORTHERN CALIFORNIA

INTRODUCTION

Northern California is not a homogenous area. While most of the population lives close to the San Francisco Bay area, there are also rural communities along the coast, in the mountains, and in the high desert. The location of railroads which were built to serve this part of the state were built all over the region and reflect its diversity.

Similarly, the rail-trails which have been built on the abandoned railroad grades reflect this diversity in geography and population density. There are very urban bike paths in places like Palo Alto and Berkeley. There are also remote mountain trails in the Sierras and the Forest of Nisene Marks on the coast.

Those seeking wooded trails to explore should visit the Bizz Johnson Trail, Old Railroad Grade, Loma Prieta Grade, West Side Rails, West Side Railroad, Sugarpine Railroad, Lands End Trail, Creek Trail, Tomales Bay Rail-Trail, Merced River Trail, or the Western States Pioneer Express Trail.

For those seeking paved routes for many types of recreation, try the Chico Airport Bike Path and Midway Bike Path (both in Chico), Fairfield Linear Park, Joe Rodota Trail, Tiburon Lineal Park, Sir Francis Drake Bikeway, West County Trail, San Ramon Valley Iron Horse Trail, Lafayette/Moraga Trail, Larkspur Path, Mill Valley-Sausalito Bike Path, Monterey Bay Coastal Trail, Paradise Memorial Trail, or Sacramento Northern Trail.

Whatever your interests, enjoy the beauty and benefits of rail-trails and do your part to insure that more are developed.

1: LANDS END TRAIL

Endpoints: Beach House to Cliff House
Length: 1.2 miles
Surface: dirt/sand
Original Railroad: Ferries and Cliff House Railroad, built 1884, abandoned 1925
Restrictions: NMV, no horses
Location: Fort Mason, San Francisco, San Francisco County
Manager: National Parks Service

Directions: To get to the east end, take Geary Boulevard going west and turn right on Thirty-third Avenue and left on El Camino Del Mar. Park alongside the road. The trail is on the ocean (north) side of El Camino Del Mar. To get to the west end, take Geary Boulevard to Forty-eighth Avenue. The rail-trail is to the right and slightly west of this intersection.

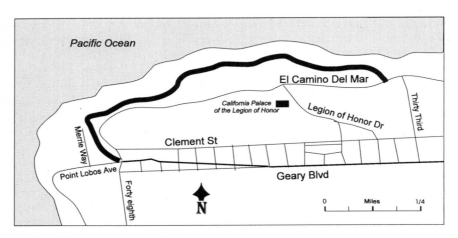

Description: The Lands End Trail provides one of the most spectacular views of the San Francisco Golden Gate Bridge as it clings to the crumbling cliffs above the ocean. You will also have views of the Marin Peninsula and out across the Pacific Ocean. The trail is about 500 feet above the water and you can hear the waves crashing on the rugged, rocky coast line below.

The railroad which operated here had a most unusual beginning. It was started in 1884 by Adolph Sutro who wanted to make the Cliff House and Sutro Heights more accessible for the working class people of San Francisco. He built a very expensive railroad that only charged riders one nickel with free transfers to other lines. The entire route took twenty minutes. He later built a separate line down Clement Street. At the peak this line had six locomotives and twelve coaches. The cost of rebuilding the railroad finally spelled its demise and it ceased operations on February 7th, 1925 after the 30th landslide.

Starting at the west end, the trail begins as a smooth dirt surface, wide and away from the sea above the Cliff House Restaurant. As it turns east around the cape called Lands End the trail deteriorates. The railroad was closed because of major landslides and the slides continue today. Several bad landslides have made the trail a steep narrow track improved with steps in many places. The eastern section (1/2 mile) is not suitable for even the most skilled mountain bicyclist due to the steps placed there to help prevent further erosion.

This is a great place on warm, clear days for a view of the ocean and the Golden Gate Bridge. There are plans to continue a beach level trail along the coast to the Golden Gate Bridge.

2: OLD RAILROAD GRADE

Endpoints: Blithedale Park to parking area and lookout
Length: 8 miles
Surface: original ballast/rock
Original Railroad: Mt. Tamalpais and Muir Woods Railway, built 1896, abandoned 1930
Restrictions: NMV, no bicycles on top mile
Location: Mill Valley, Marin County
Manager: Marin Municipal Water District

Directions: You will probably want to start at the bottom of this trail although you can drive to the parking area near the summit. To get to the bottom trailhead, take the Blithedale exit from State Highway 101 and continue up Blithedale through the center of Mill Valley until the road becomes very narrow and shaded with trees. Here you will find Blithedale Park, a small turnout. The railroad grade is on the left side of the creek going uphill and in two hundred yards it crosses the road. The trail is marked with a large gate with user restriction signs on it.

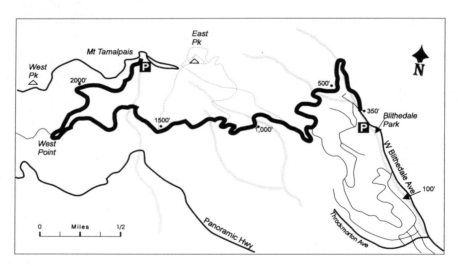

Description: Breathtaking views and a steep climb typify the Old Railroad Grade up Mt. Tamalpais. You may wish the trains were still running as you climb to the top, but you will have plenty of time to reflect on the glory years when railroads were the only means for civilized folks to get out into the "wilderness."

This is a steep rail-trail, climbing from 300 feet to 2200 feet over a distance of 8 miles. This is a gradient of between 4% and 6% most of the way, with a maximum pitch of 7%. The trees are fairly large and provide a good deal of shading on the lower portion. However, during warm days you should make sure you have adequate water. At 1.8 miles the trail is now a paved road for 0.7 miles and then returns to a rough dirt/rock surface. At 3 miles you can see the remains of Mesa Station, an outpost where a horse drawn stage road came up from the west. At 4.4 miles you will cross Fern Creek which usually has water in it year round. At 5.3 miles you will come to the West Side Inn located at West Point. This inn is part of a larger building that once stood in this place and is still operational. You can stroll around inside and see old photographs of how life used to be.

The last section of trail is more exposed with dramatic views to the south and east. At 7.1 miles there is a parking area where the paved road meets up with the trail. There are picnic tables, restrooms, and sometimes a food vendor. The trail to the summit is steeper and no bicycles are allowed. However, on a clear day the view is spectacular looking east across San Francisco Bay and south to San Francisco.

This railroad was built purely for taking tourists to the top of Mount Tamalpais. Because the grade was so steep, shay engines were used that had geared drives. This railroad was quite famous at the height of its use. The book, *The Crookedest Railroad in the World*, explains the entire history of this railroad and can be found in the large bookstore in the center of Mill Valley or ordered from your local bookstore.

3: MILL VALLEY-SAUSALITO PATH

Endpoints: Mill Valley to Sausalito
Length: 3.5 miles
Surface: asphalt with parallel crushed stone
Original Railroad: Northwestern Pacific Railroad
Restrictions: NMV
Location: Mill Valley, Marin County
Manager: Marin County Department of Parks

Directions: To access the north end, from State Highway 101 take East Blithedale Avenue west to Lomita Drive and turn right. The trail parallels Lomita Drive. Go north to the school and park there. The unpaved railroad grade continues ¼ mile further north to the south entrance of the Alto Tunnel which is blocked. To get to the southern end, take the first exit going northbound on State Highway 101 over the Golden Gate Bridge to Sausalito. The trail begins at Gates Road off of Bridgeway. The trail is first recognizable at Dunphy Park at Napa Street in Sausalito.

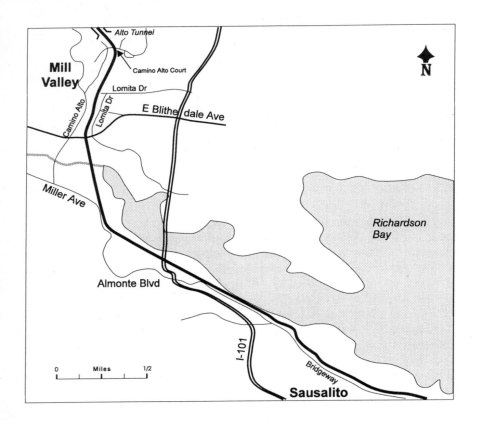

Description: The Mill Valley-Sausalito Path is a wonderful way to traverse a very car-oriented urban area. This rail-trail takes you from the un-populated hills of Mill Valley to the noisy tourist-filled Sausalito.

Starting from the extreme north end at the closed Alto Tunnel, the first ¼ mile is unpaved. It proceeds alongside a quiet neighborhood to East Blithedale, a major arterial. Just south of East Blithedale the trail crosses a large tidal delta of Richardson Bay. This is a great place to watch birds and to be out in the open away from most roads and cars. There are additional trails heading out across the marsh.

The trail continues around the bay and goes under State Highway 101 and parallels it to Bridgeway, a side road to the Golden Gate Bridge. From here to Sausalito only portions of the route are still on the railroad grade although this may change in the future. Walkers are best advised to use the sidewalk on the east side of Bridgeway and cyclists are recommended to ride on Bridgeway -- negotiating the traffic is better than trying to ride three foot wide sidewalks with trees planted in the middle.

In Sausalito you will find an old abandoned railroad car which indicates that the trains once ran on this route. You will also find a concentration of shops and places to eat. Bicyclists may want to continue south along Bridgeway to the base of the Golden Gate Bridge.

The Mill Valley-Sausalito Path is part of a proposed Cross Marin Bike Path. Detailed plans have been completed to develop several segments of this route.

4: LARKSPUR PATH

Endpoints: Alto Tunnel to Bon Air Road
Length: 1.25 miles
Surface: asphalt/dirt
Original Railroad: Northwestern Pacific Railroad, trail built 1990 and 1994
Restrictions: NMV, no horses
Location: City of Larkspur, Marin County
Manager: City of Larkspur

Directions: To get to the southern end, from State Highway 101 take the Tamalpais Drive exit and head west for 3/4 of a mile. After an "S" turn, turn left into Menke Park and continue straight through the parking lot on Monocito and follow Monocito until you see the trail at the same level on your left. To get to the north end, from State Highway 101 take the Sir Francis Drake Boulevard exit westbound. Turn left on Bon Air Road and go south ¼ mile. When you cross the Madera Creek you will see the trail on the south side of Bon Air Road.

Description: The Larkspur Path was built from a short segment of an old commuter railroad through this suburban neighborhood. The name of the community actually derives from the Lark's "spur" line which split from the Northwestern Pacific's main line that went east from the Baltimore Station.

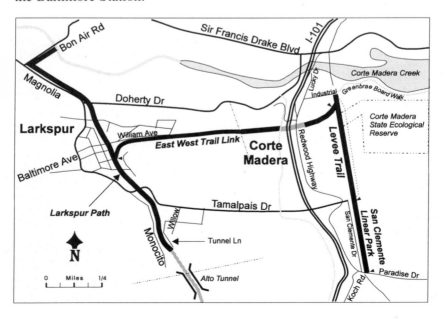

The trail starts just north of the Alto Tunnel alongside Monocito. This segment is actually located in the City of Corte Madera. The Alto Tunnel was once part of the railroad route. It is closed now but someday may be re-opened for light rail, perhaps with a trail overhead. As the trail heads north it is unpaved until it comes to Menke Park. Carefully cross Tamalpais Drive and go through a new parking lot built on the old railroad grade. From here north the trail is paved. This segment to Baltimore Avenue was completed in 1994. Just to the east at Baltimore Avenue in the trees is the relic of the Baltimore Station, an electric generating plant used by the railroad. The land to the east has been recently purchased and will be kept as park land for the future. The main line turned east here into Corte Madera (see East West Trail Link) and this section also will be improved as a trail in the future.

Heading north from Baltimore Avenue, the trail passes beneath large trees in the back yards of homes. Next it enters a congested area where you will find a small railroad station stop converted for use by local business people. Where the separated trail stops, follow the road across Doherty Drive and onto the sidewalk on the east side of Magnolia. Either stay on the sidewalk or take the two looping paths to your right which go out to the waterfront around new housing developments. Turn right on Bon Air Road and look for the path to cross Bon Air Road just before the Corte Madera Creek. From here there is a narrow path which goes upstream alongside the creek.

There are plans to make the southern portion of this trail a part of the Cross Marin Bike Path going from the north end of the Golden Gate Bridge north to Novato and the county line.

5: EAST WEST LINK TRAIL

Endpoints: The Levee Trail to Larkspur Path
Length: 1 mile
Surface: gravel
Original Railroad: Northwestern Pacific Railroad
Restrictions: NMV
Location: Corte Madera, Marin County
Manager: City of Corte Madera

Directions: From State Highway 101, take the Redwood Highway exit going northbound. Turn left on the Redwood Highway for two blocks and right on Industrial. Go two blocks east to the north end of the Levee Trail. Head south on the Levee Trail and take the trail which angles off to the right (west). To get to the west end, follow the directions for the Larkspur Path and head east from the Baltimore Station.

(See map page 42.)

Description: The East West Link Trail is just what its name implies, it connects two other rail-trails in the Corte Madera/Larkspur area of Marin County. This segment used to be part of the main line of the Northwestern Pacific Railroad. While its primary duty now is to connect two local trails together, it may eventually be a significant link in the Cross Marin Bike Path which will go from Sausalito to Novato.

This trail is not completed but you can use portions of it. The portion from The Levee Trail to the Redwood Highway is open although it is a rough gravel path. The section of the grade under State Highway 101 is still being used by a private company. The canal crossing has not been fixed since the canal construction removed some of the railroad grade. The section from the canal to the Larkspur Path is in good condition with a gravel surface. This path is away from most development with great views out to the bay. The City of Corte Madera owns most of the undeveloped land on both sides of this trail to the west of the canal and so it is likely it will stay undeveloped.

6: *LEVEE TRAIL*

Endpoints: Paradise Drive to Corte Madera Creek
Length: 0.75 miles
Surface: asphalt/dirt
Original Railroad: Northwestern Pacific Railroad
Restrictions: NMV
Location: Corte Madera, Marin County
Manager: City of Corte Madera

Directions: To get to the south end, from State Highway 101 take the Tamalpais Drive exit eastbound. Turn south on San Clemente Drive and turn right onto Paradise Drive where you can park on the street. To get to the north end, take the Redwood Highway exit from State Highway 101 and turn left (north). Take the first right onto Industrial and go east two blocks. The trail begins here.

(See map page 42.)

Description: The Levee Trail is a great place from which to view the wildlife in the Corte Madera State Ecological Reserve to the east. It also provides an excellent route for a walk or a connecting bicycle ride between the south end of Corte Madera and the north end.

Starting at the south end the trail is a meandering paved path alongside busy San Clemente Drive. This section is called the San Clemente Linear Park. From Tamalpais Drive north the trail is gravel. To the west is a pond that was probably created by the construction of the railroad grade. Although called the Levee Trail, the real levee is fifty feet to the east. There is also an informal narrow dirt trail on the top of the levee which provides a better view to the east across the undeveloped land. Towards the north end of the trail is the eastern end of the East West Trail Link. Currently you can only travel on the East West Trail Link to the Redwood Highway.

The trail ends at the north at Industrial Street. There are plans to extend the trail across the railroad bridge over Corte Madera Creek. Currently, to cross the creek you must follow a circuitous route. From the north end of the Levee Trail at Industrial, turn left (west) and go two blocks to Lucky Drive. Turn right on Lucky Drive and keep to the west side. There is a two foot wide paved path which leads to a freeway exit bridge over Corte Madera Creek. Carefully use the sidewalk of this bridge and go over the creek. At the bottom of the north end of the bridge go through the gap in the concrete railing and proceed to the path intersection. The path east goes out to the ferry dock. The boardwalk leads back west under State Highway 101 and to a paved trail along the north bank of Corte Madera Creek.

The northern portion of this path and the crossing of the Corte Madera Creek would be part of the Cross Marin Bicycle Path. The southern portion would provide access from Tiburon and Belvedere. When the East West Trail Link is completed, you will be able to travel to the Larkspur Path.

7: TIBURON LINEAL PARK

Endpoints: Blackie's Pasture to Mar West Street
Length: 2.3 miles
Surface: asphalt
Original Railroad: Northwestern Pacific Railroad
Restrictions: NMV, no camping, no fires, pets on leash
Location: Tiburon, Marin County
Manager: City of Tiburon

Directions: To get to the west trailhead, take State Highway 101 to State Highway 131 (Tiburon Boulevard) and go east one mile to Blackie's Pasture Road. Turn right and immediately left into the parking area named Richardson Bay Park operated by the City of Tiburon. To get to the east end, continue along State Highway 131 into the shopping area of Belvedere. The trail begins on the south side of the road on a sidewalk just west of the last business on Mar West Street.

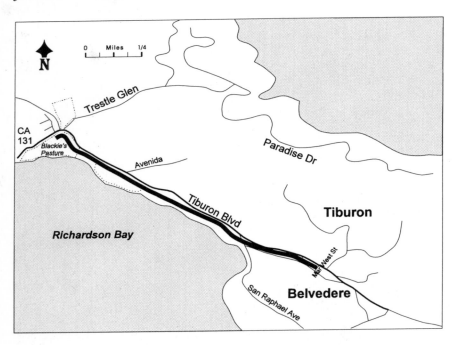

Description: The Tiburon Lineal Park is built on former Northwestern Pacific Railroad right-of-way which ran from Corte Madera through a long tunnel to Tiburon. It provides an outstanding walking and bicycling route with fantastic views of Sausalito, the Golden Gate Bridge, and Mt. Tamalpais. Thanks to the preservation of the old railroad grade, anyone can share the same views as the wealthy homeowners of Belvedere and Tiburon.

Starting at the west end, the trail passes by a sewage treatment facility that is home to the Max H. Grefe Wildlife Sanctuary, small wildlife ponds managed by the Richardson Bay Sanitary District. There is drinking water and restrooms next to the ponds.

The trail splits with the paved portion climbing steeply uphill to the railroad grade. The lower gravel path continues along below a large grass field then circles up to regain the upper path. Further east is a small children's playground sheltered from the frequent winds. The trail then parallels close by the smooth San Francisco Bay shoreline providing an unobstructed view southwest to Sausalito. You can even catch a glimpse of the Golden Gate Bridge and Mt. Tamalpais in the distance.

Close to Tiburon the trail narrows alongside the road and combines into the sidewalk near the Tiburon shopping area. The trail ends at Mar West Street. Look up the hill to see an historic church high on the hill about ¼ mile north.

When the railroad was operating, Tiburon was the north bay terminus for the barges that transported the railroad cars across San Francisco Bay. It was a major port through World War II but now is only used for a ferry to Angel Island.

8: SIR FRANCIS DRAKE BIKEWAY

Endpoints: Tocaloma to Shafter Bridge
Length: 3.4 miles paved, 1.9 miles unpaved, 5.3 miles total
Surface: paved/gravel
Original Railroad: North Pacific Coast Railroad, built 1874, abandoned 1933
Restrictions: NMV
Location: Samuel P. Taylor State Park, Golden Gate National Recreation Area, Marin County
Manager: California Parks Service, Pt. Reyes National Seashore

Directions: From State Highway 101, take Sir Francis Drake Boulevard 15 miles west to Samuel P. Taylor State Park. You can access the trail in the park. The west end can be reached by continuing through the park to the intersection of Sir Francis Drake Boulevard with Platform Bridge Road, the site of a former town called Tocaloma. Immediately after turning off Sir Francis Drake Boulevard onto Platform Bridge Road there is an old highway bridge to your left across the Lagunitas Creek which takes you to the trail. There is some parking along Platform Bridge Road. The east end cannot be easily accessed. The closest parking is at the Irving Group Picnic Area, east of the main park entrance.

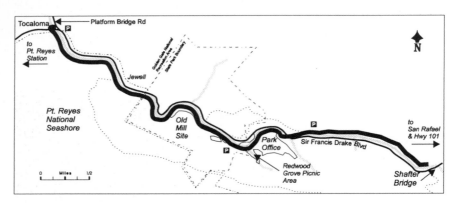

Description: The Sir Francis Drake Bikeway is a delightful trail among the tall trees next to Lagunitas Creek. The gentle railroad grade makes walking and bicycling easy. This trail also creates a bypass for bicyclists traveling through the area who want to avoid the narrow highway.

Starting at the west end (Tocaloma), the trail is paved and runs close alongside the Lagunitas Creek beneath cool, dark trees. At 1.4 miles it passes out into a broad meadow where the Jewell Trail takes off uphill and climbs 0.9 miles to the Bolinas Ridge Trail which is open to mountain bicycling. At 2.2 on the bikeway there is a small bridge over the creek where you can get to the highway. At 2.4 miles the trail becomes an access road for the state park.

At 3.4 miles the trail turns to gravel and at 3.9 miles crosses on a foot-bridge over the highway. This is also a popular starting location but has limited parking. The trail continues another 1.4 miles until it ends at a missing trestle over the creek. If the water level is low in the creek you can take a side path to the south which crosses the creek to get back to the highway at Shafter Bridge, otherwise return the way you came.

The park is named after Samuel Taylor, a businessman who operated a paper mill just west of the current park headquarters. The first narrow gauge line passed by his mill in 1874. He saw all the people passing by on the train and subsequently established one of the first outdoor camping areas in the United States.

The northern part of this trail is managed by the Point Reyes National Seashore and the southern portion by the California Parks Service. Get a good brochure about this area from the Samuel P. Taylor State Park information booth. It shows the many other trails open for hiking, bicycling, or horse back riding. There is a day fee for use of the park.

This trail follows the route of the North Pacific Coast Railroad which went from Larkspur to Cazadero, north of the Russian River. Many portions of the right-of-way are intact. The Pt. Reyes National Seashore owns much of the grade between Tocaloma and Pt. Reyes and has plans to improve it. Portions of the line along Tomales Bay are in good shape but parts have washed away. This could be part of a great trail going north to the Russian River. There are also some plans to improve segments to the east along the railroad right-of-way.

9: TOMALES BAY RAIL-TRAIL

Endpoints: Pt. Reyes Station to Millerton Point
Length: 3 miles total
Surface: dirt
Original Railroad: Northwestern Pacific Railroad, abandoned 1933
Restrictions: NMV
Location: Pt. Reyes Station, Marin County
Manager: Point Reyes National Seashore,
California Parks Service

Directions: This trail is not well used and requires some exploration to find. Take State Highway 1 north to Pt. Reyes Station. Follow State Highway 1 north to where the highway approaches the bay. At the top of the first hill looking north across the bay is a Pt. Reyes National Seashore parking area. Park here and take the trail heading west down across a field by following the sign posts. This trail eventually reaches the railroad grade. The segment to your right (north) is open but does not connect completely across the bay. The Millerton Point segment can be reached by continuing north on State Highway 1 to a small parking area at Millerton Point.

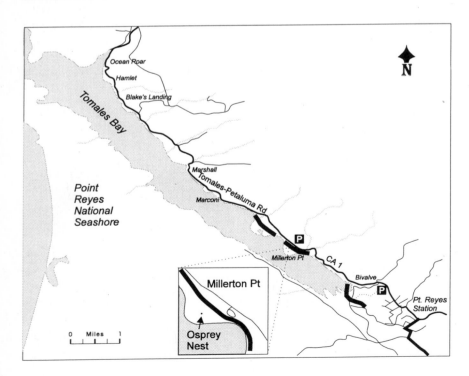

Description: The Tomales Bay Rail-trail is in the process of being created. Currently there are two segments open and accessible although they are very primitive. The surface varies and may be covered with brush or be quite wet. Conditions aside, the adventurous are rewarded with a quiet, uncrowded place to explore part of the railroad which ran from Sausalito all the way north to Cazadero, north of the Russian River.

The southern segment is accessible via a path across a pasture and down a hill to the bay. This is a great place for birding or just getting away from the roads which are close to both sides of the bay. There is a great view looking northwest up the length of Tomales Bay. But the best views are of the prolific wildlife which lives in the inter-tidal zones. The best time to explore is at low tide. The railroad grade used to have a small bridge over the outlet to the creek which needs to be replaced.

The second location to explore is at Millerton Point. Here there is a parking area for several cars and a path close by an osprey nesting pole erected for just such use. The rail-trail is located between the parking lot and the trail to the osprey nest. To the north it is in a shallow draw. To the south the grade goes out across the shallows and ends where there is a break in the grade. The accompanying photo is taken from the south looking north along this segment. The osprey nest is the pole in the far left of the photograph.

To the north of Millerton Point is a large peninsula managed by the Pt. Reyes National Seashore. The railroad bed goes across this peninsula although it is not improved. Contact the Pt. Reyes National Seashore for more information about access. This segment begins immediately north of the Tomales Bay Oyster Company which has fresh oysters for sale.

10: WEST COUNTY TRAIL

Endpoints: State Highway 12 to State Highway 116
Length: 1 mile
Surface: asphalt
Original Railroad: Northwestern Pacific Railroad, trail built 1994
Restrictions: NMV
Location: Sebastopol, Sonoma County
Manager: Sonoma County

Directions: Take State Highway 116 to Sebastopol. Turn right on State Highway 12 and turn north across from the old railroad station onto Morris Street. Go north on Morris Street to where it turns west. The trail begins on the north side of the road and heads west.

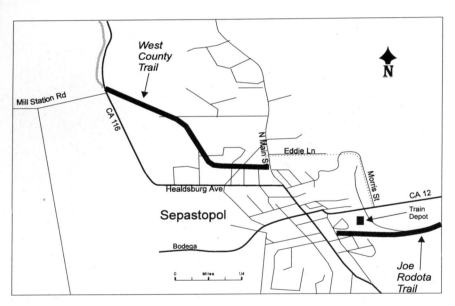

Description: The West County Trail is the second segment of a planned trail system across Sonoma County that would go from downtown Santa Rosa to the Russian River. It is just north and west of the first segement, the Joe Rodota Trail, and provides a scenic route through a residential area of Sebastopol.

The route begins on Morris Street as a signed bike route from State Highway 12. Where Morris Street turns to the west there is a short segment of separated trail that connects Morris Street with Eddie Lane. Watch for cars along Eddie Lane. Also, watch out for the children who use this lane to get to the school on the south side.

Cross North Main Street and go 100 feet south to where the trail continues on the railway grade. The railroad turned south here and ran down the middle of Main Street. Heading west, the trail enters a residential neighborhood. Mature oak trees shade the trail on hot days. The grade was built up on the ridge and few roads cross the grade. It is a quiet place and extremely popular with local residents.

Further west you will pass by orchards on both sides. Please do not pick the fruit and stay out of the private orchards. The open orchards are a contrast with the deep woods of the residential area to the east. The trail ends at State Highway 116. There are plans to continue north alongside the highway up to the Russian River.

11: JOE RODOTA BIKE TRAIL

Endpoints: Santa Rosa to Sebastopol
Length: 3 miles
Surface: asphalt
Original Railroad: Petaluma and Santa Rosa Railroad, built 1904, abandoned 1986, trail built 1990
Restrictions: NMV
Location: Santa Rosa, Sonoma County
Manager: Sonoma County Regional Parks

Directions: The west end of the trail is in Sebastopol at the intersection of Highways 12 and 116. Go 1 block south to Burnett and park in the parking lot. The trail starts just east across Petaluma Avenue. To get to the east end, take State Highway 12 towards Santa Rosa and turn right on Merced Avenue. There is parking for a few cars immediately on your right.

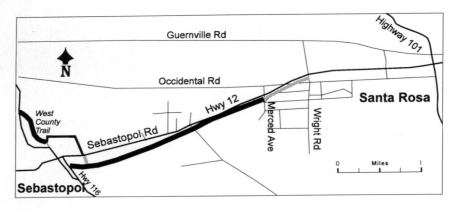

Description: The Joe Rodota Bike Trail parallels busy State Highway 12 between Santa Rosa and the small town of Sebastopol. It passes through farm land and across several small creeks and provides a wonderful scenic trip between the two communities.

The best end to start at is in Santa Rosa at Merced Avenue. While the trail is parallel to State Highway 12, it is far enough away that you will feel very much in the country. There are views across the agricultural lands to the south and north and occasionally a low flying airplane from the airport to the south. Stop and pause at the bridge over Laguna de Santa Rosa Creek before continuing into Sebastopol. The trail ends on Petaluma Avenue. One block north and two blocks back east on State Highway 12 is a unique building, the old railway depot complete with three passenger cars and a refrigerator car. This is the location of the former repair yards and it now houses various shops.

This trail was named for a former director of Sonoma County Regional Parks. The county definitely plans to make a connection between this trail and the West County Trail which starts in Sebastopol and goes north. There are also plans at the east end to extend this trail through the center of downtown Santa Rosa.

12: SONOMA BIKE PATH

Endpoints: Fourth Street East to Sonoma Highway
Length: 1.45 miles
Surface: paved
Original Railroad: Northwestern Pacific Railroad, abandoned early 1970's
Restrictions: NMV, no horses, dogs on a leash
Location: Sonoma, Sonoma County
Manager: City of Sonoma

Directions: To get to the west end, from State Highway 101 take State Route 116 (near Petaluma) east. Turn left (east) on Stage Gulch Road (State Route 116), right (south) on Arnold Drive (State Route 116), left (east) on State Route 121, and left (north) on State Route 12. The west access is directly across from the Maxwell Farms Regional Park next to the "Big O Tires" sign. To get to the east access take State Route 12 to West Spain Street. Travel east on West Spain Street which turns into East Spain Street to Fourth Street East. Turn left (north) to Lovall Valley Road next to the Sebastiani Vineyard's tasting room. The trail starts between the rows of grapes.

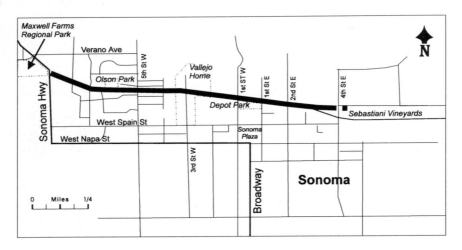

Description: Situated in the middle of the northern California wine country, the beautiful Sonoma Bike Path rail-trail passes through a vineyard and past a historic restoration of old California history. You will find plenty of parks and places to visit along the trail.

Starting from the east end at Fourth Street East and Lovall Valley Road, the trail begins by passing between perfectly clipped grapevines of the Sebastiani Vineyards. You get the feeling that you are in the middle of the farm and you are. At Second Street East on the north side is "The Patch," an informal local outlet for the huge garden of fresh vegetables grown next to the trail. Just south of the trail is a wonderful cheese factory, the Vella Cheese Company located in the Sonoma Brewing Company building. If you continue two more blocks south off the trail you will find The Plaza, a shaded park taking up an entire block with wonderful old hotels and shops all around.

Returning to the trail at Second Street East is the beginning of a Par Course which goes west along the trail. Next along the trail is Depot Park which has an old restored train depot operated by the Sonoma Valley Historical Society. It is open Wednesday through Sunday, 1:00 - 4:30 pm. There is also picnicking, ball fields, and a children's playground. After Depot Park the trail passes through a wide open grassy field. On the right is the road leading to Lachryma Montis, former home of Mariano G. Vallejo, a Mexican general who built the house in 1852. Here you will find restrooms, a picnic area, a small museum, and a pond used to raise fish. Continuing west you will pass Olsen Park, a small community park with a basketball court and children's playground. Further west the trail winds between newer homes until it reaches State Route 12. Across State Route 12 is another park, the Maxwell Farms Regional Park. Be sure to use the crosswalk to cross this busy street.

There are plans to extend this trail at both ends. On the east end the railroad curves south and is abandoned down to Schellville, a small highway intersection. To the northwest there is some right-of-way still available to continue north for three miles to Agua Caliente.

13: MONTEREY BAY COASTAL TRAIL

Endpoints: Pacific Grove to Seaside
Length: 7 miles
Surface: cement/asphalt/dirt
Original Railroad: Southern Pacific Railroad, abandoned 1979, trail built 1986
Restrictions: NMV, no horses
Location: Monterey, Monterey County
Manager: City of Monterey, City of Pacific Grove, City of Seaside

Directions: To get to the east end, take State Highway 101 south to Seaside. Follow Del Monte Avenue through Seaside keeping the railroad to your right. The trail begins where the rails have been removed. To get to the western end, take State Highway 1 south and turn right on State Highway 68 to Pacific Grove. State Highway 68 becomes Sunset Drive. The trail starts at the intersection of Sunset Drive and Crocker Avenue in Pacific Grove and heads north.

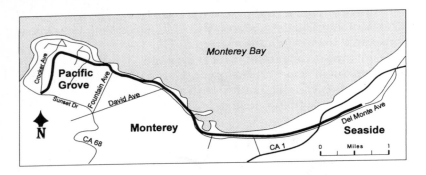

Description: The Monterey Bay Coastal Trail is a wonderfully scenic route that traverses three different beach communities. Pacific Grove is a quiet residential community, Monterey is a crowded tourist town, and Seaside is a working community. You can target your visit to enjoy the entertainment and dramatic seascapes in Monterey or avoid the crowds and still enjoy a long walk or bicycle ride along the coast.

The best place to start is from the west at Sunset Drive and Crocker Avenue in Pacific Grove where you can still see the rails in the road surface. Going north the trail passes through a very quiet residential area with huge trees and a grass covered right-of-way. Keep your eyes open for the tame deer which frequent this area.

At 1.3 miles the trail turns sharply to the right. Go left on the next paved road which crosses the grade to avoid a golf course. Turn right on Ocean Boulevard and stay on this road until you enter the Monterey City limits at 2.5 miles. Here the trail is right along the waterfront lined with shops and food establishments. At 3.2 miles you will pass by Cannery Row and the Aquarium, two major attractions in Monterey. It can be very congested in this area, especially on weekends in the summer. Watch out for the 4 and 6 person pedal-powered surreys that take up half the trail.

There are numerous tourist attractions on the Monterey waterfront. Sample them as your interests dictate. As for railroad history, the only evidence you will find is in the two old railway cars used as information centers and a post office. Amidst the crowded commercial scene, take the time to admire and appreciate the rugged, rocky coast line.

Beautiful views of the rocky coast are available all along the route and north of all the stores is a beautiful public beach with palm trees and white sand beaches. Beyond the Monterey city limits the trail continues north another unpaved one-half mile into Seaside. Just north of Seaside is a separate paved trail which continues all the way to Castroville and, maybe someday, all the way to Santa Cruz. The railroad to Castroville may be abandoned for interstate commerce, but there is interest in keeping it operational for light rail to Santa Cruz.

14: LOMA PRIETA GRADE

Endpoints: Loop Trail within Nisene Marks State Park
Length: 6.7 miles (round trip)
Surface: dirt
Original Railroad: Loma Prieta Railroad, built 1910, abandoned 1922, trail built 1978
Restrictions: NMV, foot traffic only, closed dark to 6 am
Location: Aptos, Santa Cruz County
Manager: Nisene Marks State Park, California Parks Service

Directions: From State Highway 1 take the Aptos exit. Cross over State Highway 1 and right on Soquel Drive. Turn left before the Aptos Station on the Aptos Creek Road. The entrance to Nisene Marks State Park is straight ahead. Note: the park is closed from dark to 6 am.

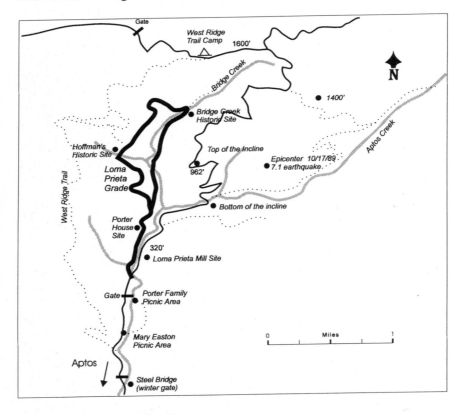

Description: The Loma Prieta Grade is located in a beautiful forest with a tremendous history. For many reasons, the forest was left undisturbed for a long time. This is very rugged country located on earthquake faults. The Ohlone Indians who first inhabited this region avoided the particular area because it was difficult to traverse. The original Spaniards passing through in 1769 found it unsuitable for grazing or farming, their primary interests. The Aptos and Hincklay Creek watersheds are so steep that 19th century surveyors chose to stay on the ridge tops for their surveys. Only when the Loma Prieta Lumber Company finally purchased this valley in 1881 was the forest threatened. The sight of huge redwood trees made them willing to overcome obstacles that had deterred previous visitors. The lumber company teamed up with Southern Pacific Railroad and together they pushed a standard gauge railroad line seven mile up Aptos Creek with numerous trestles. To get the logs to the railroad they used oxen, steam donkeys, high lines, skid roads, inclines and hard work. They managed to push into every canyon in the watershed during their 40 year ownership and removed a staggering 140 million board feet of lumber. The logging stopped in 1922. No more trees were left standing. The last rails were pulled in 1931. The 9,600 acres were purchased in the 1950's by the Marks family and donated to the State of California in 1963 in memory of their mother, Nisene Marks.

Now that it is preserved as a state park, this area has come a long way towards recovering its former grandeur. This trail provides a loop trip through a deep forest where one can simply walk quietly and observe nature or explore the sites of old railroad logging activity. As you travel back into the woods, you can feel the forest thicken and the air darken. One can only imagine the size of the redwood trees before man cut them down. If you look carefully you can still find some of the original stumps.

While the trees continue to grow, the land is still changing. In the springs of 1982 and 1993 flood waters roared down these creeks washing away many of the old trestles and railroad grades. On October 17, 1989, the epicenter of a 7.1 magnitude earthquake was measured near the center of the forest.

Note that there is a permanent gate at the Porter Family Picnic Area. No motorized vehicles are allowed past this point. While the Loma Prieta Grade is closed to bicycles, you may choose to ride from the picnic area (or from Aptos) to the trailhead ¼ mile north, but take along a bike lock. You may hike but not bicycle from the trailhead and explore nature and railroad history. The state park manager has a good brochure on this area with more history and trails identified.

15: BOL PARK BIKE PATH

Endpoints: Hanover Street to Arastradero Road
Length: 1 mile
Surface: asphalt
Original Railroad: Southern Pacific Railroad
Restrictions: NMV
Location: Palo Alto, Santa Clara County
Manager: City of Palo Alto

Directions: To get to the west end, from Interstate 280 take the Page Mill Road exit and go north on Page Mill Road. Turn right (east) onto Porter Drive. Porter Drive turns left (north) and becomes Hanover Street. Just before Hanover turns to the west you will see on your right a narrow gap between a large building and a parking lot. This is the western terminus of the trail. To get to the south end, take the Arastradero Road exit from Interstate 280. Go to the south side of the high school and look for a paved path leading west.

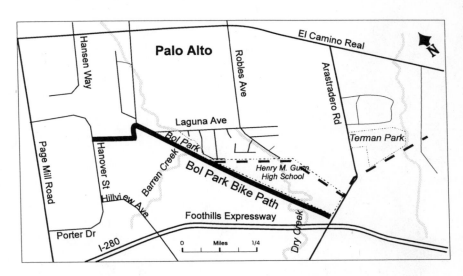

Description: The Bol Park Bike Path is an example of an urban railroad right-of-way which now provides a narrow path through a populated area. Commuters, students going to school, and residents going for a quiet walk all find this a popular route for winding through the community. It is part of the comprehensive bike path system of Palo Alto.

Starting from the west, go through a narrow gap and come out at Bol Park where the trail gains the railway grade. This is a quiet narrow park amidst a residential area and north of a business park. The trail crosses Barren Creek on a high bridge and emerges alongside an open meadow before crossing Dry Creek. At the Henry M. Gunn High School the railroad route goes behind (west) of the ballfield until it reaches Arastradero Road. You can continue south on a short trail by going left on Arastradero Road about one block and finding a narrow trail on the south side of Arastradero Road across from the high school entrance. This short trail continues ¼ mile further southeast to Los Altos Avenue. Beyond Los Altos Avenue there is one unpaved block before the trail ends.

Palo Alto has good bicycle facilities. From the east end of the Bol Park Bike Path at the high school, you have several options for continued travel. To go south, you can take a separated bike path along Arastradero Road. There are also on-street bicycle routes north on Arastradero, east on the Foothills Expressway, or west on Miranda. You may also want to enjoy Bryant Street Bicycle Boulevard, a street modified for bicycling. To get to Bryant Street from the west end of the trail, continue on Hanover west to California and turn right on California to Bryant.

16: *LOS GATOS CREEK TRAIL*

Endpoints: Los Gatos to Lexington Reservoir
Length: 1.8 miles
Surface: dirt/gravel
Restrictions: NMV, dogs on leash, 15 mph for bicycles,
7 am to dusk, no fires
Location: Los Gatos, Santa Clara County
Manager: City of Los Gatos

Directions: Take State Highway 17 to Los Gatos and take the Saratoga Avenue exit eastbound. Turn right on Los Gatos Boulevard and continue south. Los Gatos Boulevard turns into East Main Street. Just before crossing a bridge over the freeway is a steep access trail on the south side of the bridge which goes down to the Los Gatos Creek Trail.

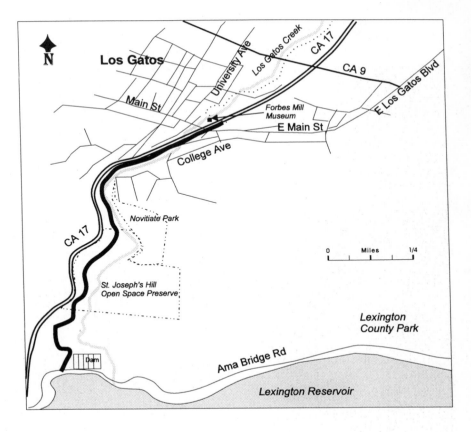

Description: The Los Gatos Creek Trail, when finished, will extend from Lexington Reservoir to the San Francisco Bay. Only the segment from Los Gatos to the reservoir is located on a railroad grade. The grade that you will see is a small section of one that ran from San Jose to Santa Cruz. The original railroad used to run through the middle of Los Gatos between Santa Cruz Avenue and University Avenue.

At the north end, the trail begins at a steep descent from the East Main Street bridge. It follows an access road built next to the Los Gatos "creek" which at this point has been placed in a deep concrete channel. In about 0.4 miles the trail goes up to the right and gains the original railroad roadbed. To the left the creek is flowing in its natural channel and there is heavy vegetation on the opposite bank. At about 1.2 miles the trail again goes steeply uphill to the right. If you look straight you can see where the original roadbed crossed the creek on a missing trestle. At the base of the dam for the reservoir the trail jogs sharply to the right and then climbs up an extreme (walking only) gravel slope to the top of Lexington Reservoir. The original roadbed is buried deep under Lexington Reservoir.

Going north on the trail under East Main Street you will come to the historic Forbes Mill Museum, open Wednesday through Sunday from 12-4 pm with displays about the history of the area and the railroads. A trail is being constructed north of the museum on the west side of the freeway by cantilevering over the steep bank sloping down to the freeway.

The rail-trail is a small portion of the entire Los Gatos Creek Trail which is being developed north to the San Francisco Bay. There is some discussion about trying to make a connection between Lexington Reservoir and Santa Cruz using the old railroad grade. This would be an outstanding scenic trail that passes through several tunnels through the mountains.

17: CREEK TRAIL

Endpoints: Penitencia Creek Road Entrance to
Aguague-Penitencia Creek Junction
Length: 1.8 miles
Surface: asphalt/dirt
Original Railroad: Alum Rock Line, built 1880, abandoned 1932,
trail built 1932
Restrictions: NMV, closed dusk to 8 am, no running of horses
Location: Alum Rock Park, San Jose, Santa Clara County
Manager: City of San Jose

Directions: From State Highway 101 take the Alum Rock Avenue exit. Follow this road east up a long hill and it will take you directly into the park. Follow the windy road down into the canyon and turn right once you have crossed the creek. Park at the end of the road in the large parking lot. The Visitor Information Center is across a foot bridge over the creek to the south.

Description: Alum Rock Park is the oldest municipal park in California, created in 1872 by the city of San Jose. Located in the mountains above San Jose, it is blessed with a year-round creek and mineral springs. By 1890 it had become a nationally know health spa which continued to serve people until 1932. An electric railroad was built specifically to take residents and visitors from San Jose up to this popular park. Today, the Creek Trail, built from this abandoned railroad line, is a great place for a quiet walk.

Start at the visitor center located in the mid-canyon area and explore the displays on wildlife, vegetation, and history. Take one of the center's regular tours or pick up a copy of their excellent brochure and guide yourself through the many trails in the park. When you are ready to explore the rail-trail, walk downstream south of Penitencia Creek.

The trail starts out on the former narrow gauge grade west alongside the creek. Stay on the trail next to the creek as it wanders downstream. You will pass under a concrete trestle which is still standing over the creek. The trail you are on is the original railroad line which was frequently flooded. Follow it out to the Penitencia Creek Road Entrance.

On the way back, look for where the upper grade crossed the creek. You can see the concrete foundations still standing on both sides. Take the trail on the north side of the creek which climbs a short distance to the grade. Eventually, you will cross over the same concrete trestle you walked under earlier and return back into the shade alongside the creek near the visitor center.

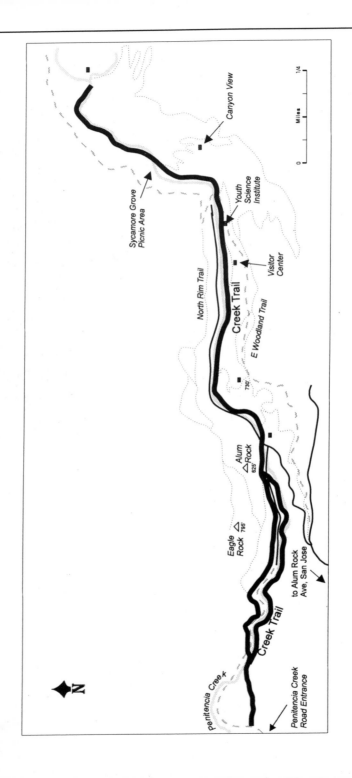

Canyon View

Youth
Science
Institute

Sycamore Grove
Picnic Area

Visitor
Center

North Rim Trail

Creek Trail

E Woodland Trail

730'

Alum
△ Rock
625'

Eagle △
Rock 795'

to Alum Rock
Ave, San Jose

Penitencia Creek

Creek Trail

Penitencia Creek
Road Entrance

N

Miles

0   1/4

The trains only ran up the creek as far as the visitor center. However, there is a good path system that continues up the creek. There are numerous stone structures and bridges to explore or sample the spring waters brought to the surface for your enjoyment. This is a popular place for rest and relaxation. When you are ready for more strenuous activity, hike the more than 13 miles of trails in this park. The biggest problem in this park is that it is loved to death. Please stay on the trails, do not litter, and do not take anything in the park home. Alum Rock Park is so popular that, in order to avoid damage, careful, respectful use by its many visitors is required.

18: SANTA FE GREENWAY (Ohlone Greenway)

Endpoints: Berkeley to El Cerrito
Length: 3.75 miles
Surface: asphalt
Original Railroad: Santa Fe Railroad, trail built 1981
Restrictions: NMV
Location: Albany, El Cerrito, and Berkeley,
Contra Costa County
Manager: Cities of Albany, El Cerrito, and Berkeley

Directions: To get to the south end, take the University Avenue exit from Interstate 80 in Berkeley. Go east to Sacramento and turn left two blocks to the Bay Area Rapid Transit (BART) station. The route

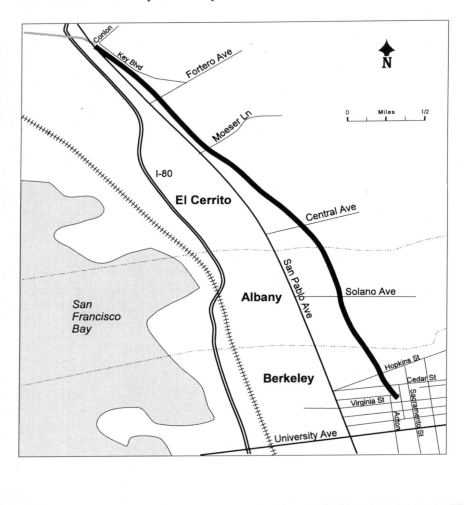

begins behind the BART station at the intersection of Virginia and Acton. Park on the street. To get to the north end from Interstate 80, take the San Pablo Avenue exit and head south. Turn left on MacDonald Boulevard and right on Key Boulevard. The route begins at the intersection of Key Boulevard and Conlon with parking along Key Boulevard.

Description: The Santa Fe Greenway is a good example of a rails-with-trails project. The old railroad grade is now shared by BART and a trail. BART is either elevated or below ground providing ample space for this popular trail.

Starting from the south at Acton and Virginia in Berkeley, the rail-trail starts out with BART located underground. The rail-trail shares the right-of-way with parks and tennis courts. There is a paved pathway that goes through these areas north to Peralta. At Peralta, turn left and immediately right onto Hopkins. In 100 feet at Gilman you will see the bike route sign on the left leading back onto the right-of-way where BART comes out of the ground.

BART is located overhead from here north on large concrete pillars. There is a wide area below the dual tracks which has been landscaped. There are two trails, one narrow, winding one for foot traffic, and one eight foot straight path for cyclists and other wheeled users. Because most of the buildings were built facing away from the tracks, they do not really impact the trail users' experience. This section is in the town of Albany and also includes a circuit training course. At Brighton Street the trail enters El Cerrito where the trail is called the Ohlone Greenway. It passes close to an operating lumber mill and then at Schmidt enters the Dinosaur Forest, a section of trail with small dinosaur statues.

Further north the trail passes close by the Hill Street BART station. The end of the trail route is at the intersection of Conlon and Key. There are plans to try and continue the route north although it would have to cross busy San Pablo Avenue.

19: SHEPHERD CANYON BIKE TRAIL

Endpoints: Montclair Shopping Center to Saroni Road
Length: 1 mile
Surface: asphalt/dirt
Original Railroad: San Francisco-Sacramento Railroad
Restrictions: NMV
Location: Oakland, Alameda County
Manager: City of Oakland

Directions: To get to the west end of the trail, take Moraga Road to Montclair, a small shopping area. Turn uphill (east) on Medau and go two blocks to the street end. The trail starts up a ramp going left below a concrete retaining wall. The east end of the trail is where Saroni Drive turns off of Shepherd Canyon Road.

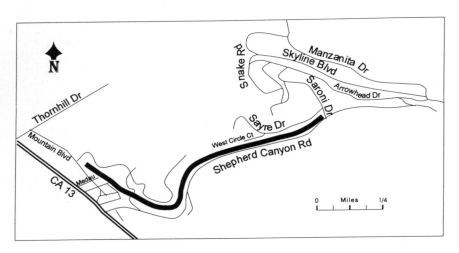

Description: The Shepherd Canyon Bike Trail saves bicyclists a narrow and steep climb up part of Shepherd Canyon Road. Its grade is much easier and it offers a beautiful scenic peek of Oakland. It is an example of how an old railroad grade can provide a gentler route in a very steep residential neighborhood.

Starting at the Montclair shopping area, look for a steep paved access path at the east end of Medau which leads up to the railroad grade. The trail crosses a bridge over Snake Drive with access to the road. Just beyond is a viewpoint with a peek-a-boo view of Oakland to the southwest. Beyond the viewpoint the trail makes a gentle curve east and continues uphill. Young trees have been planted to help beautify the trail and signs have been placed to help you identify the various species. This rail-trail is a very popular place for people who want to take a walk away from the steep, narrow roads in this area.

Further uphill the pavement ends and there is a very short dirt section (passable on road bikes) which passes through a housing development which was never completed. The rail-trail then ends although there is a paved path adjacent to Shepherd Canyon Road for the next 1/8 mile. The average grade of the rail-trail is between 2 and 4% which compares to some sections of Shepherd Canyon Road which are as steep as 6%. The railroad which used this line used to continue on to Moraga. Perhaps some day this trail will continue east to the Lafayette/Moraga Trail.

20: LAFAYETTE/MORAGA TRAIL

Endpoints: Lafayette to Moraga
Length: 7.75 miles
Surface: asphalt
Original Railroad: San Francisco-Sacramento Railroad,
trail opened 1976
Restrictions: NMV
Location: Lafayatte and Moraga, Contra Costa County
Manager: East Bay Regional Park District

Directions: To get to the north end, take State Highway 24 to
the south Lafayette exit (Pleasant Hill Road). Turn right on Olympic

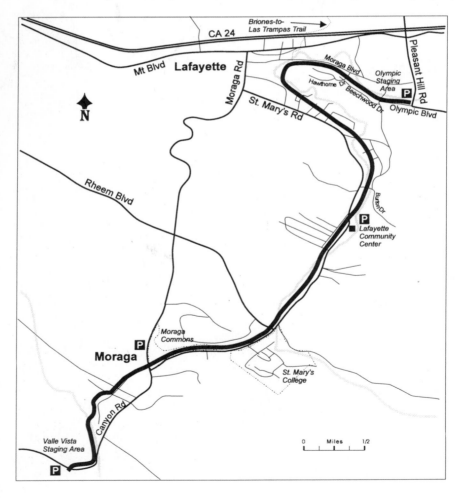

Boulevard and park in the Olympic Staging Area. To get to the south end, continue west on Beechwood Drive, right on Hawthorne Drive and left on Moraga Road. A few blocks west, turn left again on St. Mary's Road through Moraga. At Moraga turn left on Canyon Road and go about one mile south to the Valle Vista Staging Area, a gravel parking area.

Description: The Lafayette/Moraga Trail is a wonderful rail-trail that winds through a suburban area east of the Bay area. It connects one small bedroom community to another with parks and open space lands.

Starting from the north end you will find parking and restrooms at the parking area called the Olympic Staging Area. The trail winds west near downtown Lafayette. At 4th Street is a connection with the Briones-to-Las Trampas Trail which runs north. The Lafayette-Moraga trail curves back south and passes through a quiet residential neighborhood.

At about 3.5 miles you will pass the Lafayette Community Center with restrooms, parking, water, and information. Two miles further south the trail passes through the small community of Moraga. You will find food, restrooms, parking, and information at the Moraga Commons on your right at the intersection of St. Mary's Road and Moraga Road. Beyond Moraga the trail parallels Canyon Road out into the country.

This trail was first opened in 1976 and has become quite famous as an example of how a rail-trail provides a popular recreation and commuting route in a rural/suburban area. A majority of use of this trail is by people walking, with only about 20% of all users bicycling. It is heavily used by those who live nearby with more than 400,000 users per year. While the rail-trail ends now at the Valle Vista Staging area, the original railroad continued further south, making it possible that someday this rail-trail may connect to Berkeley.

21: SAN RAMON VALLEY IRON HORSE TRAIL

Endpoints: Concord to San Ramon
Length: 10.5 miles
Surface: asphalt
Original Railroad: Southern Pacific Railway, built 1892, abandoned 1978, trail built 1986-present
Restrictions: NMV
Location: Concord, Alamo, Danville, and San Ramon, Contra Costa County
Manager: East Bay Regional Park District

Directions: To get to the north end, from Interstate 680 take the Monument Boulevard exit and go east on Monument Boulevard 0.5 miles. Turn right on Mohr Lane just past the creek crossing. There is an old railroad trestle to the south of Monument Boulevard. The trail begins on the south side of the boulevard. To get to the south end, from Interstate 680 take the Alcosta Boulevard exit. Go east on Alcosta Boulevard two miles and turn left on Pine Valley Road. Go west 0.5 miles and the trail will be on your right. The section south of here is unimproved.

Description: The San Ramon Valley Iron Horse Trail is a long rail-trail built through a fast growing suburban area in the San Ramon valley, east of Oakland. It was a difficult trail to construct because the rail-line had been abandoned for a number of years and some of the grade was already being developed. This is a great place to go for a long ride or walk, with plenty of interesting places to stop along the way.

From the north, the trail starts at Monument Boulevard and heads south. In 0.5 miles there is a section of trail which may not be completed. Detour by turning east on Hookston, continuing south on Bancroft, and then right on Mayhew back to the trail. Continue south 0.3 miles to another gap in the trail. Jog west and use Coggins Drive which parallels the missing segment. Get back on the trail at Treat Boulevard. Just south of Treat Boulevard 0.1 miles is the intersection with the Briones-to-Mt. Diablo Trail which goes both east and west. South of here is a long straight segment to Valley Road. At Valley Road you will need to take South Broadway Avenue for one mile until you see the trail begin to the south across from the Broadway Plaza. Here the trail passes through a rather open area and underneath Interstate 680.

The next segment passes behind a residential area with plenty of trees. You will pass Alamo Plaza on your left and continue into Danville. The railroad grade runs right through the busy middle part of Danville and there are plenty of shops and places for food and drink. There is also

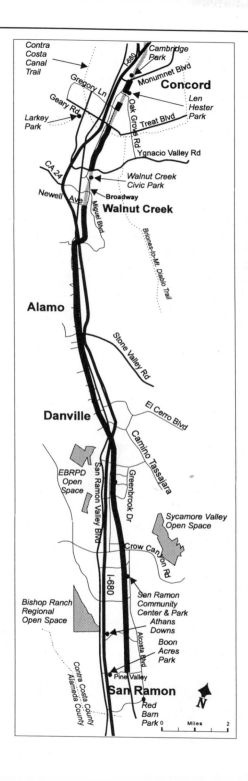

an old railway station which is being restored. Watch for the trail signs which lead you across San Ramon Valley Boulevard and pass again under Interstate 680. A mile south of Interstate 680 is Sage Park next to the trail, a pleasant place to relax. The trail south passes through a dense residential area. It is another 4.7 miles south to the end of the trail at Pine Valley Road in San Ramon.

In 1890, local farmers had difficulty getting their crops to market on poorly constructed muddy roads. They got together and donated land to the Southern Pacific Railroad Company and were able to get a railroad built through the San Ramon and Diablo Valleys. Work on the rail-trail began in 1982 with a grant from the state legislature. The trail's success is due in part to the efforts of a local citizen group, the Right of Way Trail Advocates. The first trail segments were opened in 1986 with more segments being added every year.

If you are not familiar with the area, the East Bay Regional Park District (EBRPD) provides a wonderful trail map showing details and mileage for all segments. You can obtain a copy from the trail manager listed in Appendix 1. The EBRPD has plans to continue the trail north to Suisun Bay and south to Pleasanton.

22: BLACK DIAMOND MINE TRAIL

Endpoints: Black Diamond Mine Regional Park
headquarters to mines
Length: 1 mile
Surface: dirt
Original Railroad: Pittsburgh Railroad, built 1866, abandoned 1949
Restrictions: NMV (not passable when surface of trail is wet)
Location: Antioch, Contra Costa County
Manager: East Bay Regional Park District

Directions: From State Highway 4 take the Sommersville exit. Turn south up Sommersville Road and follow it to the park headquarters buildings in the hills to the south. The rail-trail is the dirt path to the left of the paved road directly south and uphill of the buildings.

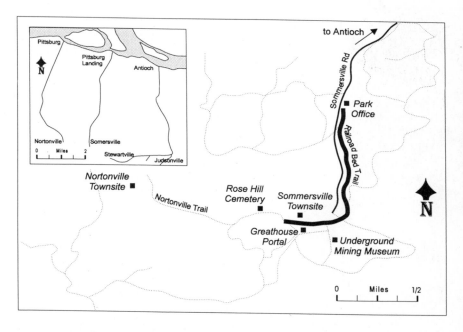

Description: The Black Diamond Mine Trail begins at Sidney Flats, the location of the park headquarters. The trail begins directly south of the headquarters buildings through a closed gate. It parallels the paved road and after a half mile the original grade heads off to the right. You can see the partially exposed timbers of the trestle over the creek where the weather has eroded the earth. Continue straight on the trail which will lead you to the mine entrance.

The first railroad in this area was the Pittsburgh Railroad built in 1866 using light weight standard 47 gauge rail. The railroad operated from the dock at Pittsburgh to the mining town of Sommersville, a distance of 5.3 miles. The lower sections had grades of 1% but through the canyon the grade was up to 5.2% with sharp curves, one 350 foot long tunnel and numerous trestles, one which was 304 feet long and 60 feet high. In order to reduce maintenance problems with the trestles, the railroads gradually filled in the trestles with mine tailings over the years. This process protected the trestles from fires. Erosion now has exposed some of these fills so that you can see the original trestle timbers. The full mining cars were coasted down to the docks and the engine used only for hauling the empties back up to the mine.

At one time there were five major coal mining towns in this area which were the major coal producers for all of the San Francisco area. Between 1860 and 1900 nearly four million tons of coal were removed fueling California's move from a rural to industrial base. To accommodate this amount of activity, two other railroads were constructed in the area, Black Diamond Coal & Railroad Company and the Empire Coal Mine & Railroad Company. Some of the mines were re-opened between 1920 and 1949 to mine fine sand used in glass making and in the Columbia Steel Works in Pittsburgh.

This is an interesting park to explore, with beautiful grassy slopes, historical sites, and scenic vistas. An important attraction of this area is a mine tour which is offered by park staff. The mine tour is a great place to go, especially on a hot day. There are 34 miles of trails, native and exotic plant species, the Rose Hill Cemetery, and of course, the sand mine tour. The park headquarters building located at Sidney Flats has historic photos and brochures describing the history of the region.

23: FAIRFIELD LINEAR PARK

Endpoints: Solano College to Travis Boulevard
Length: 4.5 miles
Surface: asphalt/concrete
Original Railroad: Sacramento Northern Railroad
Restrictions: NMV, no horseback riding
Location: Fairfield, Solano County
Manager: City of Fairfield

Directions: To get to the east end, from Interstate 80 east of San Francisco take the Travis Boulevard exit and head east about 1/2 mile. Turn left into the Solano Mall and park. The trail begins directly west across Travis Boulevard. To get to the west end, take the Abernathy Road exit from Interstate 80 and go north. Turn left on Rockville Road and left on the Suisan Valley Road. Turn left into the Solano Community College and go east to the playfield parking lot. The trail begins on the south side of the playfields.

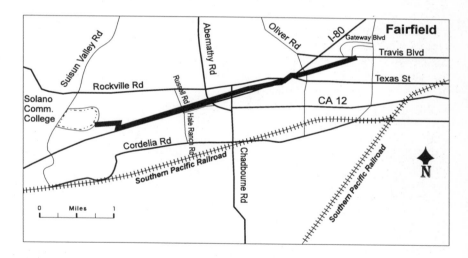

Description: The Fairfield Linear Park is a rail-trail which connects downtown Fairfield with a local community college. It provides a safe bicycle/pedestrian route alongside a busy freeway using an old railroad right-of-way.

The east end of the trail begins in the busy part of Fairfield across from a mall. It starts in a park heavily landscaped with a rose garden and a par course. There are many street crossings providing easy access to the trail from the residential neighborhoods. Further southwest are picnic benches and a children's playground. The trail is lined with lush plantings on both sides of a meandering concrete path.

At Texas Street the trail passes under Interstate 80 and begins to parallel it on the north side. Although the right-of-way is narrow here it does provide a safe route alongside the roar of Interstate 80. At the west end the trail turns northeast away from the freeway and ends at a gravel parking area at the playfields of Solano Community College.

There are plans to continue this trail east to Vacaville and points north of Vacaville. For railroad fans, the Western Railway Museum is located 12 miles southeast of Fairfield on State Highway 12.

24: SACRAMENTO NORTHERN BIKE TRAIL

Endpoints: Sacramento to Rio Linda
Length: 8 miles
Surface: asphalt
Original Railroad: Sacramento Northern Railroad, abandoned 1985
Restrictions: NMV
Location: Sacramento, Sacramento County
Manager: Sacramento Parks and Community Services

Directions: To get to the south end, from Sacramento go north on 16th Street and turn right on North B Street after passing under the main line tracks. This is an industrial area so watch where you park. The trail starts on North B Street two blocks east of 16th. This route may connect to downtown Sacramento by the time you read this. To get to the north end, from Interstate 5 take the road north to Rio Linda. In the center of town is a park and the rail-trail starts at this point and heads south.

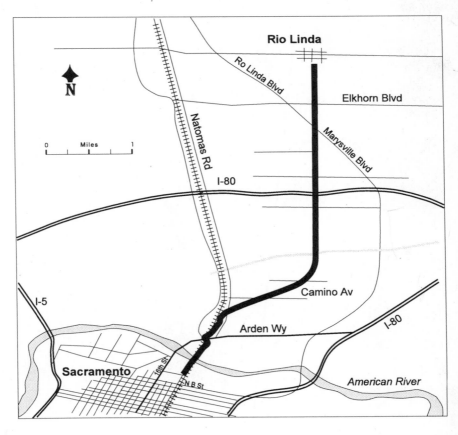

Description: The Sacramento Northern Bike Trail is a wonderful example of a rail-trail that gives city dwellers easy access to rural land. This trail route starts in downtown Sacramento and transports the trail user far out into the farmlands north of Sacramento.

The trail begins in an industrial area of Sacramento just north of the main east/west active railroad line. It climbs up to an old railroad bridge across the American River. There are great views from the bridge of the wide flat American River below. The bridge has an asphalt deck with six foot high cyclone fencing which keeps little kids safe and allows tall people to have an unobstructed view of the river. The route drops down from the trestle and comes to an intersection with the American River Trail. Turn left at this intersection marked Discovery Park and then continue straight across the first road you come to. Climb back up a hill to the railroad grade and follow this north for 1/2 mile. The trail then passes through a mixed residential/commercial area. The right-of-way was very wide through here and there is little vegetation.

As you travel north of Camino Avenue the housing becomes more scattered and there are more trees close to the trail. You are separate from cars and can travel for many miles. The trail crosses several creeks and the land is greener. At Rio Linda there is a small picnic shelter, water, grass, and a community center. There is also a grocery store and small cafe. Traveling this entire route makes an excellent bicycle ride. Walkers can walk from downtown to the bridge and back, go north from Camino Avenue, or start at Rio Linda and take a walk in the country. There are plans to continue this route further north following the old abandoned Sacramento Northern Railroad right-of-way.

25: *MERCED RIVER TRAIL*

Endpoints: Railroad Flat Campground to Lake McClure
Length: 8.5 miles
Surface: dirt/rock
Original Railroad: Yosemite Valley Railroad, built 1907, abandoned 1945, trail opened 1993
Restrictions: NMV, horses not advised
Location: Briceburg, Mariposa County
Manager: Bureau of Land Management

Directions: To access the east trail head from State Highway 49, turn east on State Highway 140 to Briceburg. Turn left across the bridge at the Briceburg Visitor Information Center and continue west to Railroad Flat Campground. The trailhead is just west of the campground. It is not easy to access the trail from the west except at very low water levels. Even then there might be a steep creek bank to cross. This approach is not advised.

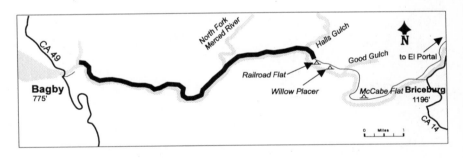

Description: The Merced River Trail is a beautiful trail along the picturesque Merced River which is listed as a national wild and scenic river. The trail is popular with hikers, mountain bicyclists, and people fishing. There are also places where they share it with those rafting down the river. The Merced River drains Yosemite Valley and its water level varies considerably. The scoured walls along the river attest to the high water levels possible.

The only realistic starting point for this trail is at Briceburg. There is no town or services, but you should stop and visit the Briceburg Visitor Information Center located there. You will learn about the history of this area and can get up-to-date information about the river and the trail.

Cross the river and continue west. The road you are on uses the railroad grade until it ends at Railroad Flats Campground. Here, uphill from the river, are four graves testifying to the longevity of this site. One is of a person who died in 1910. One grave is of a 7 year old. One grave is unmarked. The most recent is marked 1934-1991 with an epitaph for a person who regularly visited the area.

The trail starts out across Halls Gulch from Railroad Flats Campground. There is a good bridge for your use with a steel barrier that effectively keeps out all but foot traffic. You can lift a mountain bicycle over this barrier, but probably not a horse. It may be possible for horses to cross upstream from this bridge. Contact the trail manager listed in Appendix 1 before visiting for equestrian use.

The trail passes by a private residence built by a writer trying to get away from it all. Unfortunately, he picked a very popular place. Next you will see remnants of an old diversion dam used for getting water before the reservoir was built. The dam was dangerous for rafters and, after one person was killed, the dam was removed. Next comes a section of continuous rapids and a narrowing of the gorge. The trail is quite rough along here with many loose rocks and boulders.

At the North Fork there is a pullout for rafts to avoid the North Fork Falls. The old trestle across the North Fork is gone but the footings are still visible. Follow the trail upstream a short distance to a crossing which is difficult except at low water. If the water is high, you will have to continue upstream or come back when the water is lower. Note that if you do cross the river here, there is a trail on the west side of the North Fork if you climb back up to the same elevation as the railroad grade that you left.

Below the North Fork the valley is a little bit wider. Continuing on the north side, across the river you will see a creek enter from the south. From this point west the river is sometimes backed up by the reservoir and, unfortunately, the trail is being destroyed when it is submerged. At about 1/2 mile from State Highway 49 there is a creek crossing with a missing trestle. The reservoir has eroded the sides to create very steep walls. It would be difficult to go around this area by going upstream. Do not count on being able to reach State Highway 49 from the trail.

The trail officially ends at Bagby, the site of an old railroad station that is now submerged below the reservoir, Lake McClure. Situated at the intersection of the Merced River and State Highway 49, it still shows up on current maps. There is a private park and boat launch at Bagby with water access. However, it is on the south side of the river and the Merced River Trail is on the north side. The rail-trail is located along the north bank and is submerged unless the reservoir is extremely low.

In the future there are plans to open up more of the trail upstream to the public. You may explore some sections in their current condition. Taking State Highway 140 further east, the next bridge across the river is at Foresta which will give you access to the railroad grade. Between El Portal and Ned's Gulch most of the grade is passable by car. Finally, near El Portal, some of the railroad grade is used as a paved road. It is worth the visit to El Portal, the gateway to Yosemite. At the east end of "town" is the end of the railroad line, where you can find an old shay style engine and a caboose.

There are plans for Bureau of Land Managment (BLM) and the U.S. Forest Service to work together and try to extend this trail thirty miles upriver to El Portal. BLM is also considering extending the trail west to Merced. This would require a new route around the reservoir where the the railroad grade is submerged.

26: WEST SIDE RAILS

Endpoints: Hull Creek to Clavey River
Length: 10 miles
Surface: dirt
Original Railroad: West Side Railroad
Restrictions: NMV
Location: Toulumne, Toulumne County
Manager: U.S. Forest Service

Directions: From State Highway 108 turn off at Longbarn. Go southeast on Forest Service Road 3N01 for eight miles. Turn right on 3N07 for five miles, then left on 2N03 for two miles, then right onto 3N86 which is the railroad grade. In two miles you will find a parking area alongside the grade.

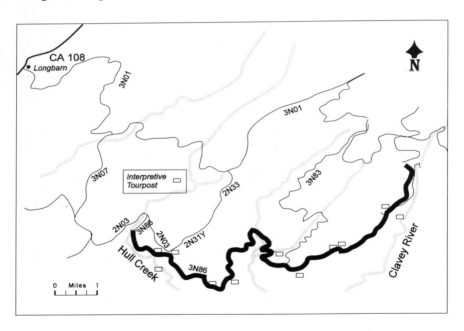

Description: This stretch of the West Side Railroad, which has been preserved as the West Side Rails, makes a wonderful route for a day trip. This trail shares the same original railroad as the West Side Railroad Grade. The undeveloped portion between these two trails is still intact and someday it may be possible to connect them.

The U.S. Forest Service has done an excellent job of interpreting the history of this railroad grade. Scattered along the route are twelve interpretive signs explaining where logging operations were located. They have also produced an excellent brochure on this trail which you can obtain at the Mi-Wuk Ranger Station.

The trail runs through the deep forest at an elevation of about 6,000 feet. There are big pine trees and in the winter it is not easily accessible because of snow. It is very rugged country and in several places where it crosses streams the bridges have washed out. You will have to wade through the creek bed at low water or come back another day if the water is too high. This trail is really out in the woods so come prepared with food, water, and emergency gear.

27: WEST SIDE RAILROAD GRADE

Endpoints: Mira Monte Road to end
Length: 2 miles
Surface: dirt
Original Railroad: West Side Railroad
Restrictions: NMV
Location: Toulumne, Toulumne County
Manager: Toulumne Parks and U.S. Forest Service

Directions: From State Highway 108 take County Road E17 south to Toulumne. Turn left on Carter Street (which after town becomes E17 again) for 0.4 miles. Turn right on Buchanan Mine Road and left on Mira Monte Road. The trail begins south of Mira Monte Road where there is some parking.

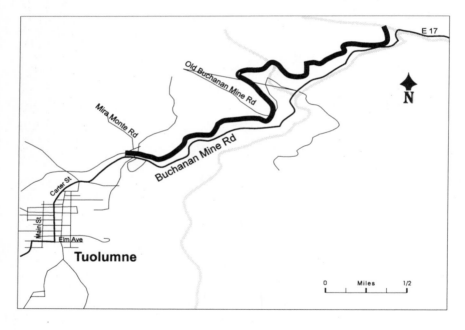

Description: The West Side Railroad Grade is a rustic trail that follows the narrow gauge route of the West Side Railroad. It is a unique rail-trail in that there are still sections of rails and ties left in place. The trail has been carved out adjacent to these railroad artifacts to provide visitors with a historical perspective and education.

The starting place for this trail is in a little draw with a steep grade, about 3%. It climbs over a hill and rounds a corner with an outstanding view to the west and south. The rail-trail traverses the steep hill. In about 1 mile a large tree provides shade and a bench has been placed beneath it for your use. In about 1.5 miles the remnants of the old rails and ties remain. At this point the trail becomes only about 12 inches wide alongside the tracks. In about 2 miles there is a tight turn through a cut with a great view up the valley to the east. You can see the route of the railroad winding along the hillside ahead of you. The grade crosses a dirt road which connects to E17 below. A few hardy explorers continue further, but use would be greatly increased if the trail were brushed. Vocal public support may make it happen. This trail is part of the same railroad corridor as the previous trail, West Side Rails, to which it may be connected in the future, again, if public support makes it happen.

28: SUGARPINE RAILWAY TRAIL

Endpoints: Fraser Flats Campground to Strawberry
Length: 2.5 miles
Surface: dirt
Original Railroad: Sugar Pine Railroad Company
Restrictions: NMV
Location: Twain Harte, Toulumne County
Manager: U.S. Forest Service, Mi-Wuk District

Directions: To get to the west end, go east on State Highway 108 past Mi-Wuk Village 9 miles. Turn left on Forest Service Road 4N01 to Fraser Flat Campground.

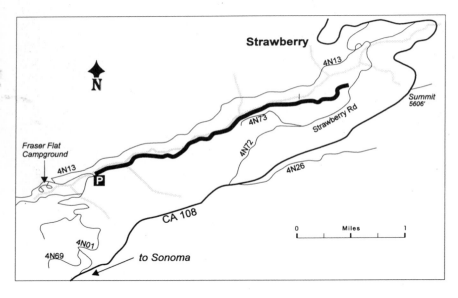

Description: The Sugarpine Railway Trail is named for a railroad built to harvest the large suparpine trees that grow in this area. This is very steep country and this rail-trail is the easiest and pleasantest way to travel here as it passes close alongside the beautiful Stanislaus River.

The best place to start is from the Fraser Flat Campground reached via Forest Road 4N01. Follow this road down to the Stanislaus River. Immediately before crossing there is a small dirt parking area. The trail begins at this point and heads upstream.

The river valley is shallow and narrow with the railroad grade close to the river. In some places the river has cut a deep narrow channel, dropping far below the rail-trail, while in others it sweeps close to the level of the grade. Look for an old wooden flume across the river and other relics of the past. In about two miles the railroad grade turns away from the river and heads uphill. When you get within sight of a private home, turn right and follow the worn trail which ends up at a paved road, Old Strawberry Road. Turn right on Old Strawberry Road to reach State Highway 108 which will take you back to the campground road (4N01) or retrace your route for a great downhill trip.

This railroad originated at Toulumne and passed through Twain Harte, Confidence, and close to Lyons Reservoir. There are many sections still intact although some are in private ownership. Ask locally or at the Forest Service about other segments which may be open for public use. The railroad grade continues far up into the mountains and would make a great route if it were continued east. There are tremendous opportunities for rail-trails in this forest where logging railroads used to abound. Citizens must ask agencies to preserve these grades and then work with Forest Service staff to close these old railway grades to motorized use in order to make them safe and enjoyable for non-motorized users. If you enjoy this trail, please get involved.

29: EL DORADO COUNTY TRAIL

Endpoints: Dimity Lane to Jaquier Road
Length: 1.7 miles
Surface: asphalt/dirt
Original Railroad: Camino Placerville and Lake Tahoe, abandoned
1986, trail opened 1992
Restrictions: NMV, daylight only
Location: Placerville, El Dorado County
Manager: El Dorado County

Directions: To get to the west end, from Interstate 50 take the Broadway exit at Placerville. Turn right (west) on Broadway and right again (north) on Mosquito Road. Turn right on Dimity Lane and in 100 yards you will pass the trail on the left. There is no parking here but you can park along Mosquito Road. To get to the east end, from Interstate 50 turn left on Broadway and go east to Smith Flat Road. Turn left for 1 mile and turn right on Jaquier Road. There is parking for five cars.

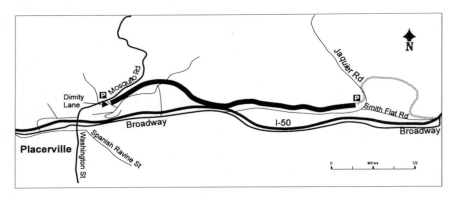

Description: The development of the El Dorado County Trail is a story in itself. A local young equestrian saw the railroad being removed and dreamed of making the right-of-way into a place where she could ride her horse. Through her vision and community help, Placerville now has a wonderful rail-trail.

Starting at the west end of the trail you will pass through a rare wood-planked, steel rib lined 100 foot tunnel. There are a few homes alongside and the trail passes close to a school. Most of the journey is through woods away from the city below. This trail is steep with 400 feet of elevation gain over 1.7 miles for a 4% grade. It climbs above and parallel to the freeway, providing an overview of town. Then it turns east and heads out into the rural land. It currently ends at Jaquier Road although the railroad right-of-way continues east up into the mountains.

Currently the rail-trail begins just north of the downtown area and continues north into the country. The abandoned right-of-way also runs south through Placerville and could be developed into a wonderful path through this narrow city. With a lot of luck and hard work, the rail-trail through Placerville and the El Dorado County Trail could be part of a continuous Sacramento to South Lake Tahoe trail.

30: WESTERN STATES PIONEER EXPRESS TRAIL

Endpoints: Auburn to Middle Fork American River
Length: 2 miles
Surface: dirt
Restrictions: NMV, no bicycles
Location: Auburn, Placer County
Manager: California Parks Service

Directions: From Interstate 80 at Auburn, take the Auburn State Highway 49 south exit. Go about 1 mile south on 49 to the bottom of the hill and proceed across the bridge. The railroad bridge is visible on the right where there is some parking available. The rail-trail goes across the bridge and uphill.

Description: The Western States Pioneer Express Trail is a dramatic rail-trail that climbs along a steep hillside above the Middle Fork American River. It is the last leg of the famous Tevus Cup long-distance horse back race.

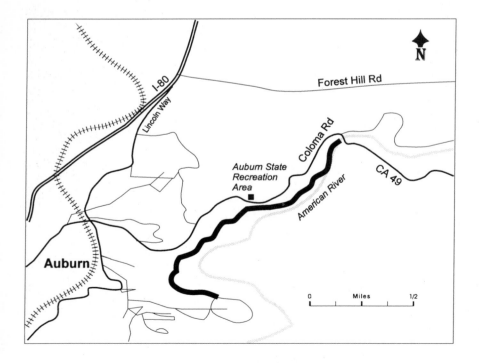

The best place to start this trail is at the American River at the old concrete bridge and head uphill. All the way to the top you can look down at dramatic views of the river canyon. There are several places where old trestles have washed away but passage is still possible. Most of the grade is wide and easy walking although you cross some of the creeks on narrow single track.

When you come to a big creek, the trail leaves the railroad grade and heads steeply uphill. In about one hundred feet you will reach a dirt road which to the left leads up to the fairgrounds in Auburn, the finish location of the horse race. To the right the dirt road leads to State Highway 49 and the park headquarters ¼ mile downhill.

The railroad grade in the canyon continues upstream for quite some distance, however, the first few miles are used as a truck road. There is an opportunity to create a rail-trail upstream after the truck road ends.

31: TRUCKEE RIVER BIKE TRAIL

Endpoints: Tahoe City to Midway Bridge
Length: 4.25 miles
Surface: asphalt
Restrictions: NMV
Location: Tahoe City, Placer County
Manager: Tahoe City Public Utility District

Directions: The best place to start on this trail is from Tahoe City, the eastern terminus. From Interstate 80 take State Highway 89 south. There are numerous places to park in Tahoe City including a parking area just south of the Truckee River crossing. The trail starts just north of the Truckee River crossing at the main intersection in town. To get to the north end, take State Highway 89 north to Midway Bridge, north of Alpine Meadows Road. Parking is permitted along State Highway 89 adjacent to the bridge crossing. Turn left and park off the highway surface. The trail begins just south of the bridge over the river.

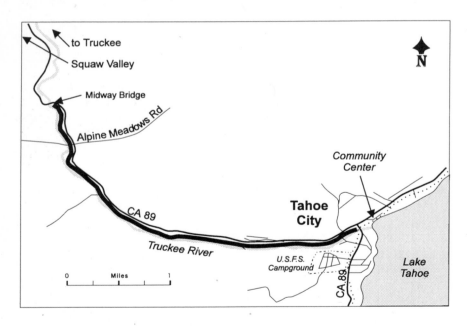

Description: The Truckee River Bike Trail is a wonderful rail-trail that parallels the Truckee River from Lake Tahoe up the river for 4.25 miles. It is wedged between the river and the State Highway 89. You travel close to the river amidst the pine trees and most of the time you tend to forget the highway proximity and just enjoy the great views.

There are no access points along the trail. However, there are a number of road crossings where you can get onto the highway. If you are visiting Tahoe City or nearby, rent bicycles or in-line skates and enjoy the trail. The gentle grade makes it ideal for beginners or novices. It is also a safe, easy place for cross country skiing in the winter. There is a paved path system that continues east and south from Tahoe City.

More than 140,000 people that use this trail between Memorial Day and Labor Day each year and this clearly demonstrates the popularity rail-trails have achieved. There are plans to continue this trail to the Squaw Valley community and resort.

32: PARADISE MEMORIAL TRAILWAY

Endpoints:	Neal Road to Pentz Road
Length:	5 miles
Surface:	asphalt/gravel
Original Railroad:	Southern Pacific Railroad
Restrictions:	NMV
Location:	Paradise, Butte County
Manager:	Town of Paradise

Directions: To get to the south end, from Interstate 5 take State Highway 32 east to Chico and then continue east along the Skyway to the town of Paradise. Pass the "Welcome to Paradise" sign and take the second right onto Neal Road. There is parking for a few cars at this point. To get to the north end, continue up the Skyway to Pentz Road. Turn right and you will cross the trail in about 50 yards.

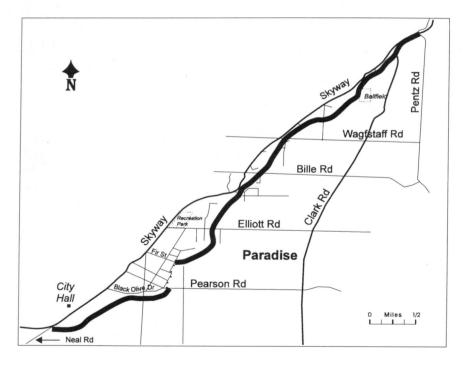

Description: The Paradise Memorial Trailway is an inconspicuous rail-trail that provides a welcome relief from the steep topography of Paradise. Gentle as it may be compared to the surrounding terrain, it is rather steep for a rail-trail, averaging around a 3% grade. The

original railroad was built by the Diamond Match Company to haul lumber from its lumber mill in Sterling down to its manufacturing plant in Chico. It was not a main line railroad so the right-of-way is quite narrow.

Start at the south end at Neal Road where there is parking for a few cars. The trail is right next to Skyway. The railroad followed a drainage which is the most gentle route in this rugged country. The first crossing is at Black Olive Road where you will need to take a detour. Take Black Olive Road north to Fir Street where you can turn right (east) and regain the grade.

The next crossing is at Elliott Road. A few blocks west is a large park and recreation center with restrooms and a picnic area. The trail then crosses Maxwell Drive, Bille Road, Wagstaff Road, Rocky Lane, Clark Road, and ends at Pentz Road.

This trail is very popular for walking. Most of the route is lined with young pine trees which shield it from city development. The entire town is built on a slope with parallel ridges and houses scattered everywhere. The trail provides one of the few places where people can stretch their legs and go for a long walk without the challenge of steep hills.

There are plans to continue the rail-trail northward for several more miles to Stirling City. This would be a wonderful route winding up into the woods to an old lumber town. It would be nice to connect this trail to Chico, but much of the original railroad grade down to Chico has been destroyed by the creation of the Skyway.

33: MIDWAY BIKE PATH

Endpoints: East Park Avenue to Jones Avenue
Length: 2.4 miles
Surface: asphalt
Original Railroad: Sacramento Northern, abandoned 1992, trail built 1995
Restrictions: NMV
Location: Chico, Butte County
Manager: Butte County

Directions: From State Route 101 in Chico, take the East Park Avenue exit and head west. At Midway Road turn left and the trail begins on your left (east) and heads south. There is some parking along Midway Road. To get to the south end, continue south on Midway Road to Jones Avenue. There is no parking at all at this intersection.

Description: The Midway Bike Path is a simple but valuable trail which goes south from the south edge of Chico. It parallels Midway Road, a very busy county road, that is narrow and has high speed traffic. The trail offers a welcome alternative route.

The trail is an eight foot wide asphalt surface with gravel surfaces on both sides. It is a great place for a long walk, a run, or a safe bypass of Midway Road for cyclists heading south out of Chico. At the north end are a few homes and then the trail passes into the country. Orchards line both sides of the trail providing fragrant blooms or enticing fruit at different times of the year. Please do not consider picking the fruit, but enjoy the fragrance and view of a productive orchard.

The primary use of the trail is by cyclists because the north end is not easily accessible on foot. There are plans to continue this trail south to the small place called Durham and possibly north to the downtown portion of Chico. There is also an opportunity to continue the trail north through Chico to connect with the Chico Airport Bike Path.

34: CHICO AIRPORT BIKE PATH

Endpoints: Esplanade to Chico Municipal Airport
Length: 1.25 miles
Surface: asphalt
Original Railroad: Sacramento Northern Railroad
Restrictions: NMV
Location: Chico, Butte County
Manager: City of Chico

Directions: To get to the south end in town, from State Highway 99 take the East 1st Avenue exit and head west. Turn right on Esplanade and go north until just before you cross Lindo Channel. Turn right on East Eleventh Avenue. There is parking along the frontage road. The trail begins just north and crosses the Lindo Channel.

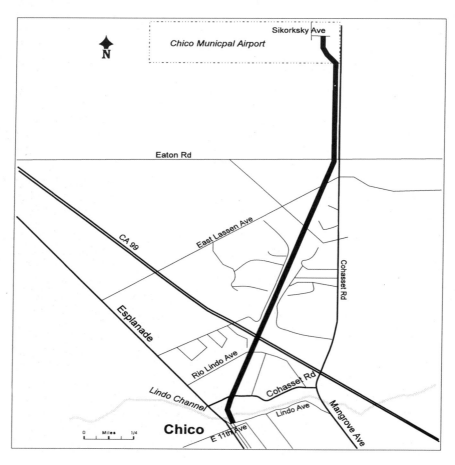

Description: The Chico Airport Bike Path is a rail-trail which transports the user from the urban area of Chico out into the country and the airport. The trail begins at Esplanade, a divided road that used to be the main road through town. The planting strip which separates the northern parallel road from Esplanade used to be the roadbed for the Sacramento Northern Railroad which ran through town. The Chico Airport Bike Path follows the route of a spur line built to the airport.

The trail first crosses Lindo Channel and passes behind many homes. The right-of-way was quite narrow creating a cozy feeling along the trail. The trail crosses Cohasset, the main road which connects to the airport. It crosses Rio Lindo Avenue and then under State Highway 99. At East Lassen Avenue the trail has a stop light which can be activated by the trail users. This is a rare example of a mid-block signalized crossing of a main road by a trail. This was made possible by the encouragement of the local bicycle community and the former mayor who is an active cyclist.

The trail crosses Eaton Road at a major intersection. Here the trail parallels Cohasset out across the open land to the airport. You will pass directly under the flight path for planes departing and arriving at the Chico Airport. The trail ends at Sikorksky Avenue at the Chico Municipal Airport where there is a covered picnic table. You can sit and watch planes coming and going.

Chico once had an electric train that transported people and goods around town. It was also the site of the Diamond National Match Company which built a railroad spur off of this line up to Sterling in the mountains. Part of that spur line is now the Paradise Memorial Trail, described previously.

35: BIZZ JOHNSON TRAIL

Endpoints: Susanville to Mason Station
Length: 25 miles
Surface: gravel/dirt
Original Railroad: Southern Pacific Fernley and Lassen Branch, built 1914, abandoned 1978, trail built 1986
Restrictions: NMV, snowmobiles permitted east of Devil's Corral during winter
Location: Susanville, Lassen County
Manager: Bureau of Land Management, Lassen National Forest

Directions: To get to the east trailhead, from Interstate 5 take State Highway 36 to Susanville. In Susanville turn right (south) on Weatherlow Street that turns into Richmond Road. Park at the Susanville Depot on your left (east). The trail begins here. Follow the railroad tracks west for ¼ mile. When the tracks end, drop down the railroad embankment on the north side and cross Lassen Street. Follow the sign up a narrow side road to the trail. To get to the west trailhead, turn off State Highway 36 at Westwood and head north on County Road A-21 for 4 miles. Turn right onto County Road 101 and go 1/2 mile. Look for the sign and a small parking area at Mason Station trailhead. Another popular trailhead is at Devil's Corral just off State Highway 36 about 7 miles west of Susanville.

Description: The longest rail-trail in California, the Bizz Johnson Trail is also one of the most beautiful. It is an excellent example of how a rural rail-trail can be an economic benefit to its neighboring communities. This trail goes from the small town of Susanville up into the pine forests of the eastern ridge of the Sierra Nevada and Cascade Mountains.

The best place to begin a journey on this rail-trail is Susanville at the Richmond Road Trailhead. Here you will find the Susanville Depot in the process of being converted to a trailhead visitor information center for all types of trails in Lassen County. It will be open Thursday through Sunday in the summer with displays of the railroad history. There is also a restored caboose that used to operate on this line. Begin your trip here heading west. The trail leaves the depot and soon enters the Susan River canyon passing over one of several bridges. To your left is an area called Hobo Camp, which describes its former use. Now it is a beautiful wooded area next to the river, ideal for picnics.

The trail winds more gently than the river and crosses the river eight times in the first seven miles. It also passes through two tunnels, one 400 feet and the other 800 feet in length. These wonderful structures provide

109

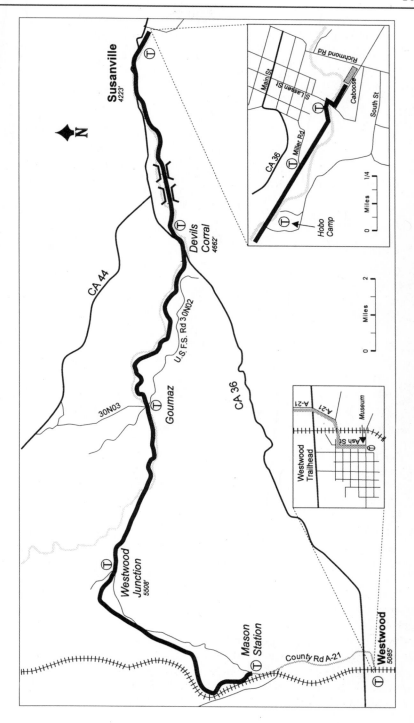

shelter in bad weather and a cool place to rest in hot weather. There are no lights in the tunnels but they are straight and, even in the 800 foot tunnel, you will always be able to orient yourself by the light at the end of the tunnel. If you prefer to avoid the dark, you will find a side path around each tunnel. The canyon walls are quite steep in this part of the canyon and climb several hundred feet up on both sides. You can see the volcanic rocks cut away by the river. The trail stays close by the river which provides nourishment in this dry climate for plants and animals.

At about 7 miles from Susanville is the Devil's Corral Trailhead with parking and a restroom. This is the last access to State Highway 36 and many visitors turn around at this point. Devil's Corral is the name for the twisted geological area where the river turns 90 degrees. Follow the trail under State Highway 36 and across a new wooden bridge built over the Susan River. Upstream from the Devil's Corral the trail passes through lush meadow before entering a pine forest. Here the land is broader and the steep cliffs are left behind. Now you will see the bounty that brought railroad tracks here in the first place, the Ponderosa and

Jefferey pine trees that grow tall. It is also open range land so keep your eyes open for cattle.

Although the trail is not steep, it does climb considerably over its 25 mile length. It starts in Susanville at 4,200 feet and gently climbs to a high point of 5,508 feet at Westwood Junction. From here it drops slightly back down to 5,272 feet at Mason Station, the western terminus. Mason Station is the physical end of the trail on the railroad grade. The official end of the trail is in Westwood, five miles south via County Roads 101 and A-21. At the small community of Westwood you will find a trail kiosk, a small museum (256-3709), and the remains of a once very busy lumber town. This was the mill town that was the center of operations for the lumber company that built this railroad.

The original railroad was created by Thomas Barlow Walker, a local private lumberman who was looking for a reliable transportation system to move his huge supply of pine lumber to market. Construction of the railroad began in April of 1913 and was completed in February 1914 from Susanville to Westwood, the mill-town built by Walker. The trail is named for a former California Congressman, Harold T. "Bizz" Johnson, commemorating his work on behalf of the trail and other public projects during the 22 years (1958-1980) he represented Northern California in the U.S. House of Representatives.

The trail has become a popular place for both local and visiting recreationists. The highest time of use is during the Rails-to-Trails Day Celebration (contact Chamber of Commerce for dates). This event features many festivities, including exciting hand car races. This event is divided into different divisions and is open to everyone. It is a chance to briefly connect with the past by pumping a real hand car. Some participants take their sport very seriously, sometimes finding sponsors and training year-round.

If you are interested in camping, the best location is to drive to Gomez which has a designated camping area. Many people also ride the trail going downhill by arranging their own car shuttle. By transporting your group to Westwood Junction, Gomez, or the Devil's Corral, you can have a shorter one-way trip with a gentle downhill grade, making it easier for all members of the group to enjoy a longer trip.

This is a long trail that is away from roads and people, one of its great values. However, trail users should be prepared and carry plenty of water and emergency gear and remember they are traveling in the mountains. If you are new to the area it is good to check in with the trail manager, the Bureau of Land Management, listed in Appendix 1. In addition to current trail conditions they have several publications that may be of interest to trail users: *The History of the Bizz Johnson Trail, Geology of the Susan River Canyon,* and *Plant Key for the Bizz Johnson Rail-Trail.* Be sure to thank them for doing such a great job in creating this trail.

36: SACRAMENTO RIVER TRAIL

Endpoints: Riverside Park to Harlan Street
Length: 4.0 miles
Surface: asphalt/concrete
Original Railroad: Southern Pacific Railroad, built 1883,
abandoned 1985, trail opened 1986
Restrictions: NMV, bicycles 10 mph, in-line skaters must
slow on tight curves
Location: Redding, Shasta County
Manager: Redding Parks and Recreation

Directions: To start at Riverside Park, from Interstate 5 take the
Central Redding/Eureka State Highway 299 W exit west for two miles.
Follow 299 W right one block and then turn left. Proceed two blocks (one
block past Market) and turn right on California. Turn left at the "T" at
Riverside Drive. Follow Riverside Drive downhill under a railroad
trestle. Before crossing the Sacramento River, turn left into Riverside
Park where the rail-trail begins.

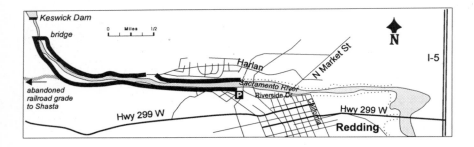

Description: The Sacramento River Trail, as its name implies, is
a trail close by the Sacramento River in Redding. It is a very popular
recreational facility for the citizens of Redding and is especially popular
for walkers and joggers. Fewer bicyclists use the trail because of the
severe speed restrictions (10 mph), although it provides a safe place for
children to learn to ride.
Begin at Riverside Park where there is parking and a trail sign. The
paved trail heads upstream on the south side of the Sacramento River.
The river is very close to the trail and is normally kept at a steady flow as
it is regulated by the Shasta Dam. There are great views across the river
and a few places to stop, sit, and relax. The smooth surface of the trail
contrasts with the rugged texture of the river banks.

At 2.5 miles upstream there is a modern stress-ribbon suspension bridge across the Sacramento River. This bridge is 13 feet wide, 418 feet long, and has 236 steel cables embedded in the concrete deck which holds it up. Cross the bridge and return downstream on a trail on the north side of the river. This trail is not built on a railroad grade which is obvious as it winds in and out among the rocks. All users must be careful of the steep grades and tight blind corners.

The paved path has a break at Harlan Street. Continue east 1,000 feet and look for the trail continuation on your right. A paved path follows along the river east to Riverside Drive. At Riverside Drive turn right across the historic Diestlehorst bridge to the park entrance across the river. This bridge has one lane of motor vehicle traffic going north-bound and the other lane is used as a two-way non-motorized route. There is also a paved path on the north side of the river that continues east from the Diestlehorst bridge and winds and jogs through Lake Redding Park downstream of Riverside Drive. The path passes under the high, curved railroad trestle and has picnic tables, restrooms, and a museum.

The Bureau of Land Management has plans to continue this trail up the Sacramento River all the way to the Shasta Dam (see Appendix 2). There is also an opportunity to complete a rail-trail along the railroad grade close to the town of Old Shasta. In 1997, the city plans to construct an 800 foot long pedestrian bridge across the Sacramento River downstream of Riverside Park which would connect with Lake Redding Park and a path along the south side of the Sacramento River.

37: HAMMOND TRAIL

Endpoints: Mad River to Murray Road
Length: 3 miles
Surface: asphalt
Original Railroad: Arcata and Mad River Railroad
Restrictions: NMV, seasonal closures at north end
Location: McKinleyville, Humboldt County
Manager: Humboldt County Parks

Directions: To get to the south end, take State Highway 101 just north of Arcata and take the Giuntoli Lane/Janes Road exit. Turn west on Janes Road for ¼ mile, turn right (north) on Heindon Road for 1.4 mile and then left on Miller Lane. Turn right on Mad River Road to the first sharp turn. The old railroad bridge over the Mad River will be directly ahead. This bridge is now open only to non-motorized traffic. The Mad River County Park with beach access is another mile along this road with some parking. To get to the north end, take the Murray Road exit from 101 and go west. When the road turns 90 degrees left (south) there is a signed trail entrance directly ahead. You can also continue south on Murray Road and take the first right on Knox Cove Road. The trail access is one block west.

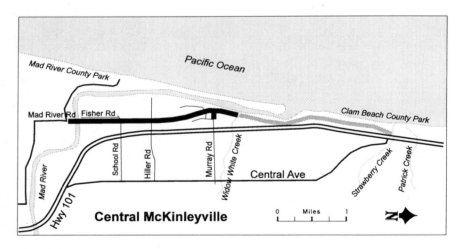

Description: The Hammond Trail is a rail-trail built on the roadbed constructed by the Arcata and Mad River Railroad. This railroad was used to transport timber from the Little River and Crannel areas to Eureka and Fairhaven. This scenic trail parallels the coast and in some places is almost in the tidal zone. It is partly paved, partly rugged, and

goes from farmland, past old cabins, through a new housing development, and right along the coast. It is a popular transportation route for people who live in McKinleyville but work or go to school in Arcata.

The trail starts at the south end by crossing the Mad River on the Hammond Trail Bridge. From the bridge there is a great view out to the beach and down into the tidal waters of the Mad River. The trail crosses farm land and climbs a short hill on Fisher Road. At 3/4 mile when Fisher Road intersects School Road is a small market and a signed alternate coastal trail bike route going east through the center of McKinleyville. Follow Fisher Road north another ¼ mile and you will see the separated trail begin again on your right (east).

Just after crossing Hiller Road you will pass Hiller Road Park with picnic sites and restrooms. The trail now passes through a very heavily wooded area all the way to Murray Road. At Murray Road the trail passes in front of some very dramatic homes and then a great view of the ocean comes into sight. The railroad was built just down from the top of the bluff and is cut into the side of the hill. The section from Murray Road to Widow White Creek is under development and may not be complete when you visit. It is separated from most homes and has a great view out to the ocean and the mouth of the Mad River.

There are plans to continue this trail north to Clam Beach County Park. Clam Beach County Park has parking, restrooms, and water. The main road north/south through this park is actually built on the old railroad grade. If you travel south on State Highway 101 from Clam Beach County Park and take the vista point turnoff you can get a great view of the mouth of the Mad River. You can also make out the path of the railroad below.

The Hammond Trail is just one link in the Coastal Trail, a project to construct a trail route along the entire coast of California.

38: *MACKERRICHER STATE PARK*

Endpoints:	Ft. Bragg to Ten Mile River
Length:	10 miles
Surface:	asphalt
Original Railroad:	Ten Mile Railroad, built 1914, abandoned 1949, trail built 1994
Restrictions:	NMV, no horses on beach south of Ward Avenue
Location:	Ft. Bragg, Mendocino County
Manager:	MacKerricher State Park, California Parks Service

Directions: To get to the north end, go to the south end of the bridge over Ten Mile River. There is a small parking area on the west side of the highway and a narrow trail leading down to the rail-trail. To get to the south end, go north from Ft. Bragg across Pudding Creek on State Highway 1. Look for a small gravel State Parks Service parking lot between two motels on your left (west). The trail begins here and heads north. Another very popular starting location is from the main MacKerricher State Park entrance. From State Highway 1, go north of Ft. Bragg about 3 miles and turn into the entrance of MacKerricher State

Park. Take the first left out to Laguna Point and park at either one of the parking lots. Those wishing to ride horses on the beach need to take Ward Avenue down to the beach. Horse back rental is available.

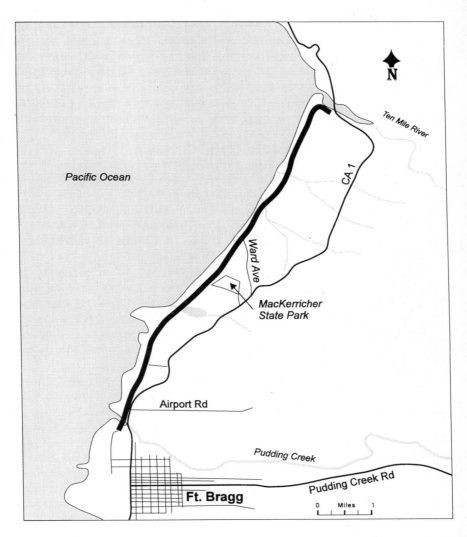

Description: The MacKerricher State Park rail-trail is a spectacular trail which runs from Ft. Bragg north along the beach. It has great views of the ocean, interesting history, and sand dunes.

The original railroad grade was built by the Ten Mile Railroad in 1914 for the Union Lumber Company's operations. It was named after the Ten Mile River and improved the ease of transporting logs to the mill near present day Ft. Bragg. In 1945 the railroad was removed and the grade converted to a road which was used by log trucks. In some places the road was twenty feet wide, but the ocean and the sand dunes have already reclaimed many portions of the trail.

The south end of the trail begins just north of a tall wooden trestle over Pudding Creek. State Parks is in the process of acquiring this trestle and has plans to renovate it and continue the trail right into Ft. Bragg. For now, the starting point is a small gravel parking area between two motels. These motels' view sides front on the trail. The trail is very popular both for visitors as well as local residents who come out for a walk or bicycle ride. Going north, the trail is soon separate from any development and is bordered by pine trees.

At about 2 miles the trail enters the Laguna Point portion of MacKerricher State Park. During the late 1800's lumber was loaded on ships at this point via a narrow dock and cables across the water to the ships at anchor. It was a very dangerous job to load the ships, especially in rough weather. Today you can walk out on the point and read interpretive signs describing the boom years. The road to the right leads to the campgrounds and park entrance. Just east of Laguna Point there is a fresh water lake, picnic tables, and restrooms.

North of Laguna Point the trail has suffered from storm damage. In some places the grade is missing entirely. The original railroad was built across the dunes and suffered from sand constantly covering the tracks. The rail-trail is no different but is not maintained to keep it free of sand. As you travel along this section you can hear and sometimes see the ocean to the west. It is a great place to rest and enjoy the scenic beauty. The trail ends at the highway bridge over Ten Mile River.

Not all of the steam trains are gone from this area. In Ft. Bragg you can ride the "Skunk" scenic railroad to Willits and back for a taste of what railroads used to sound and smell like.

39. Ojai Valley Trail
40. Fillmore Trail
41. Mt. Lowe Truck Trail
42. Duarte Bike Trail
43. Juanita Cooke Greenbelt
44. Wanda Road Park
45. Esplanade Trail
46. Newport Avenue Trail
47. Pacific Electric Bicycle Trail
48. Alton Bike Trail
49. Hoover Street Bicycle Trail
50. AT&SF Trail
51. Electric Ave. Greenbelt Median Park
52. Hermosa Valley Greenbelt
53. Faye Avenue Bike Path
54. Rose Canyon Bike Trail
55. Silver Strand Bikeway

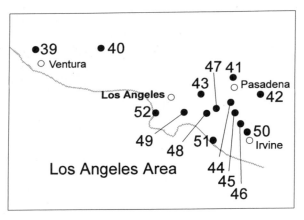

SOUTHERN CALIFORNIA

INTRODUCTION

To those who live in California, there is a strong view that the south and the north are different, almost two separate states. This difference is reflected somewhat in the nature of the rail-trails that exist in each region. Most of the rail-trails in Southern California are located in the highly urbanized areas. Often these trails are short segments of abandoned lines or wedged alongside existing lines. There are five rail-trails in Southern California located adjacent to active railroads. All these urban trails serve primarily as transportation corridors for locals on foot or bicycle. Although short in distance, they serve a vital need in these intensely urbanized areas.

In many ways, rail-trails in Southern California represent the more practical side of the trend to convert railroad grades to trails. Often, preserved railroad grades offer the only feasible route through dense urban development. Creating a single mile of unobstructed non-motorized trail in a city can represent a greater accomplishment than twenty miles of trail through open rural spaces and will be used by many more people. In a region where cars seem omnipresent and often represent the only transportation option, rail-trails offer a glimmer of hope and open space for the non-motorized traveller.

But remember, for every rule there are exceptions. If you are looking for a rural adventure in Southern California, the Mt. Lowe Truck Trail located in the hills above Los Angeles is a purely recreational trail, very rugged and scenic. And the Ojai Valley trail passes through a rural area of Ventura County.

Wherever they are found, rail-trails bring benefits to those who use them. Work to create more rail-trails of all kinds in Southern California.

39: OJAI VALLEY TRAIL

Endpoints: Foster Park to Ojai
Length: 9.2 miles
Surface: parallel asphalt and dirt
Original Railroad: Southern Pacific Railroad, abandoned late 1960's, trail opened 1987
Restrictions: NMV, dogs on leash
Location: Ventura & Ojai, Ventura County
Manager: Ventura County Parks and Recreation

Directions: From State Highway 101, take the State Highway 33 exit to Ojai. Follow State Highway 33 north to the Casitas Vista Road exit. Turn right on the frontage road and right again under State Highway 33. Turn into Foster Park and proceed to the far end of the park. The rail-trail begins on your right close to the freeway.

Description: The Ojai Valley Trail is a beautiful rural rail-trail that provides a safe scenic route from near Ventura up the Ventura River Valley to Ojai. It is best to start from Foster Park so that you will have a downhill ride on the return trip back from Ojai. You can also find food

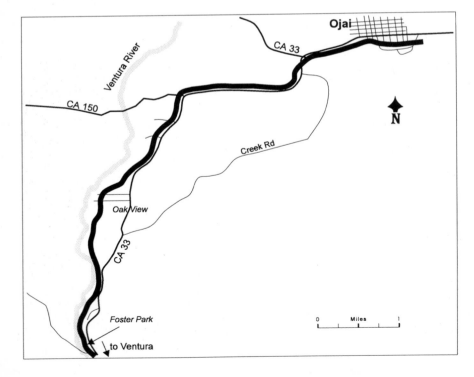

and a park in Ojai for your half-way rest stop. Or your can start at Ojai and take a shorter walking trip.

The trail starts close to the busy highway at Foster Park but soon passes behind a hill and stays close to the river bed. It passes through backyards in Casitas Springs and then crosses San Antonio Creek with a concrete ford. Note that the trail may be closed at high water due to the potential dangers of this ford. Normally the creek and flood plain of the Ventura River are dry.

From here the trail climbs moderately to attain a viewpoint over-looking the large, broad Ojai River Valley and to the northeast of the surrounding hills. For the next two miles the trail parallels and then crosses State Highway 33. Use the crosswalks when crossing this busy road. The trail then passes alongside a golf course and then through Libby Park where you will find tall trees, a creek, and picnic tables. The paved portion of the trail ends at Fox Avenue in Ojai and the dirt trail ends 0.2 miles further at Bryant Street. The center of Ojai is three blocks away on Fox Avenue. Here you will find numerous shops, a historical museum, and a bakery established before the turn of the century.

This rail-trail was well designed and planned and has been featured in a number of national stories. Underground leases to utility companies help pay for maintenance costs. It has a wooden pole fence running the entire length separating equestrian use from foot and bicycle traffic. Not only is the fence very useful and attractive, it provides a strong visual sign of the trail location. The City of Ventura has plans to connect the Ojai Valley Trail south to the Ventura waterfront.

40: FILLMORE TRAIL

Endpoints: Central Avenue to Levee Road
Length: 1 mile
Surface: asphalt/dirt
Original Railroad: Southern Pacific Railroad (active)
Restrictions: NMV
Location: Fillmore, Ventura County
Manager: Short Line Enterprises, Ltd., City of Fillmore

Directions: From State Highway 126, turn left in Fillmore on Central Avenue. Go three blocks to the town park and park on your right. The trail begins on the west side of Central just south of the tracks.

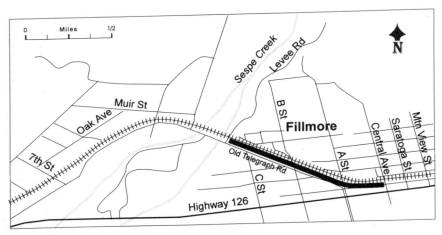

Description: The Fillmore Trail is good example of a trail alongside an active railroad. In this case, the railroad is a scenic railroad that also provides a stage for Hollywood filming. You can take a train ride and then take a walk alongside the same tracks.

The trail begins in the center of Fillmore across Central Avenue from the town park. It parallels the tracks and heads west behind the business district. At A Street the trail begins to parallel Old Telegraph Road. Here the tracks and trail pass through a residential neighborhood with housing on both sides. The trail is eight feet wide with a pole fence on both sides. There is also a dirt path on the railroad side of the trail, situated about twenty feet away from the tracks. The rail-trail is a popular route for neighborhood children going to school and it is a short, safe route for all residents to go downtown. The primary use is walking at all times of day.

Short Line Enterprises runs excursion trains on the rail line and rents its equipment out to Hollywood filmmakers. There are both diesel and steam engines. The line was originally built to haul fruit to market and it is still used for hauling fruit in season.

Fillmore is a pleasant small town nestled against the hills. This rail-trail is part of the city's plans to build a trail circumnavigating the town both for its residents and the increasing number of tourists. It is also part of the proposed Santa Clara Trail which will run from Ventura to Santa Clarita in Los Angeles County.

41: MT. LOWE TRUCK TRAIL

Endpoints: Echo Mountain to Inspiration Point
Length: 4 miles on grade
Surface: original ballast/dirt
Original Railroad: Pasadena and Mount Wilson Railway, built 1894, abandoned 1937
Restrictions: NMV, not suitable for horses
Location: Rubio Canyon, Flint Ridge, Los Angeles County
Manager: U.S. Forest Service

Directions: To get to the main trailhead, from State Highway 215 take the Lake Avenue exit and head north (uphill). Continue on Lake Avenue when it turns left and becomes Loma Alta Drive. Continue left on Loma Alta until you reach the yellow flashing light, then turn right on Chaney Trail Road. At times this road is closed due to heavy rains. It is always closed between 10 pm and 6 am. Follow this steep road to a saddle and park. The access road is gated at this point. Beyond it are two miles of steep, windy road that you need to walk or bicycle before you get to the railway grade.

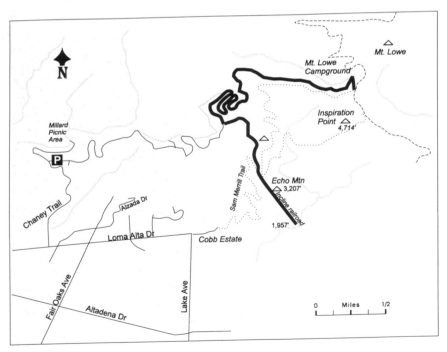

There is also a steep hiking trail which takes you to the railroad grade. Back at the turn where Lake Avenue becomes Loma Alta Drive is the entrance to the old Cobb Estate. Park off the road and walk through the deserted property and find the trailhead sign for the Sam Merrill Trail. This trail will lead you to Echo Mountain and the start of the rail-trail.

Description: The Mt. Lowe Truck Trail is a challenging trail to hike or bike because the approach is very steep. However, those who persevere will be rewarded with spectacular views and a touch of history.

Start at the Chaney Trail Road parking area where there is a small sign marking the trail head. About 100 yards uphill from the parking area is a drinking faucet and trail sign-in. The route to the rail-trail takes you

up a very steep access road that was originally built to reach the railroad grade but is now closed to motor vehicles.

In about 0.3 miles the Sunset Ridge Trail takes off to the left and roughly parallels and then reconnects with the access road in about 0.5 miles. It offers more shade and different footing than the road. The road offers views out across the Los Angeles basin.

At 1.9 miles is a junction at a saddle called Cape Hope. Off to your left is a short road which takes you to water troughs for horses and an intersection with the Sunset Ridge Trail. To your right you will find the old railroad grade which contours along the slope across the valley and ends at Echo Mountain. Echo Mountain was the top of an incline railroad and is the point where the Sam Merrill Trail comes out.

Continuing up, you are now on the railroad grade. Due to the high potential for erosion, the creek crossings are generally concrete. However, do not use this trail if it is raining or forecast to rain. This is very steep country and the water crossings can quickly become impassable.

Further up you will come to the end of the railroad. Like many railroad ventures, this one ran out of money before completion. The end point is a shaded area deep in a ravine with many of an old hotel building's foundations still intact. This is the Mt. Lowe Campground. You will usually find water here but be sure to filter before using. Continue up the road and keep right at the first intersection. The right fork takes you to Inspiration Point, the proposed end of the line.

Another route for hikers is to start from the Cobb Estate and hike up the Sam Merrill Trail. It is only two miles, but it is very steep and exposed to the sun. This slope burned in 1994 and has little vegetation. You then can hike up the railroad grade to the Mt. Lowe Campground. From the campground circle back to Echo Mountain via the Sam Merrill Trail or Castle Canyon Trail. Remember to take plenty of water as it can be very hot and dry.

Most rail-trails have little if any grade. The Mt. Lowe Truck Trail is a big exception. The railroad grade from Echo Mountain to Inspiration Point (4,714 feet) averages about 4.5 % grade. And getting to the railroad grade is even steeper. Hiking the Sam Merrill Trail from the Cobb Estate to Echo Mountain (3,207 feet) you will gain 1,250 feet in two miles, an average 11% grade. This trail is closed to bicycles and not at all suitable for horses. The paved road from the saddle on Chaney Trail Road up to the railway grade is the only route open to mountain bicycles. You had better be in good shape, have low gears, and make sure your brakes work well before you start up or attempt to come back down, since you face a climb of 1,380 feet in 1.8 miles, about a 13% grade.

This railroad vies with the Mt. Tamalpais Railroad as the crookedest in the world. There are 122 curves and 114 straight sections with the longest straight section only 225 feet long. Although most of the remnants of the railroad and buildings are gone, the memories continue. A local citizens' group led by Jim Spencer has developed a wonderful self-guided history tour about the railroad. There are numbered place markers along the route which are described in a guide book. You can obtain the guide book from the Altadena Library (600 E. Mariposa, Altadena) or from the trail manager listed in Appendix 1. You will see some railroad relics at the Echo Mountain site (railroad ties and bridge footings) and excellent narrated photographs posted along the route.

42: *DUARTE RECREATIONAL TRAIL*

Endpoints: Buena Vista Street to Vineyard Avenue
Length: 1.6 miles
Surface: asphalt/dirt
Original Railroad: Pacific Electric Railroad Co., trail opened 1978
Restrictions: NMV
Location: Duarte, Los Angeles County
Manager: City of Duarte

Directions: Take Interstate 605 north and take the Hunnington Drive/Duarte exit which is the end of the freeway. Continue straight, crossing Hunnington, and you will be on Mt. Olive Drive. At the first stop sign, turn right on Royal Oaks Drive. Immediately past Vineyard Avenue turn into the parking for Royal Oaks Park. To get to the west end, take Royal Oaks Drive west to Buena Vista Street.

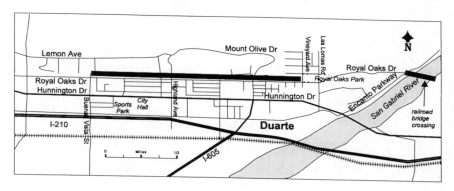

Description: The Duarte Recreational Trail is a popular urban trail in the recreation-oriented community of Duarte. Located along the base of the hills above Duarte, it is one of the older rail-trails in California and is heavily used by the local residents as a place to take a good walk, teach children how to ride bicycles, ride horses, and to commute to work. It is another example of an old railroad grade that provides one of the few public areas in a community that offers space for a continuous, uninterrupted non-motorized experience.

The trail starts at the east end at Royal Oaks Park where there are restrooms and playgrounds. The trail heads west paralleling Royal Oaks Drive. While the main trail is paved, there is also a dirt path alongside which is occasionally used by equestrians. The dirt path is separated from the asphalt path by rough posts spaced eight feet apart with no railings. This makes it easy for people to get back and forth between the two paths yet also provides a visual fence reference for horses. The trail passes under an historic stone bridge before ending at Buena Vista Street.

The original railroad continued east and crossed the San Gabriel River. Most of the grade has been destroyed between Royal Oaks Park and the river but you can continue east on Royal Oaks Drive. The old railroad bridge is still standing and is used for non-motorized crossing of the usually dry river bed.

43: JUANITA COOKE GREENBELT

Endpoints: North Berkeley Avenue to East Imperial Highway
Length: 2.6 miles
Surface: wood chips/dirt
Original Railroad: Pacific Electric Railway, abandoned 1961, trail built 1977
Restrictions: NMV
Location: Fullerton, Orange County
Manager: City of Fullerton

Directions: To reach the south end, from California 91 take the Harbor Boulevard exit north and turn left on North Berkeley Avenue. Just west on North Berkeley Avenue, across North Harbor Boulevard, is the start of the rail-trail. There is no easy access from the north.

Description: The Juanita Cooke Greenbelt is a quiet pathway through a residential portion of Fullerton. It begins at the intersection of North Berkeley Avenue and North Harbor Boulevard and heads north. East of here North Berkeley Avenue is located on the former railroad right-of-way. The trail is covered with bark chips and has a wide swath of green growing on either side which buffers trail users from the neighboring

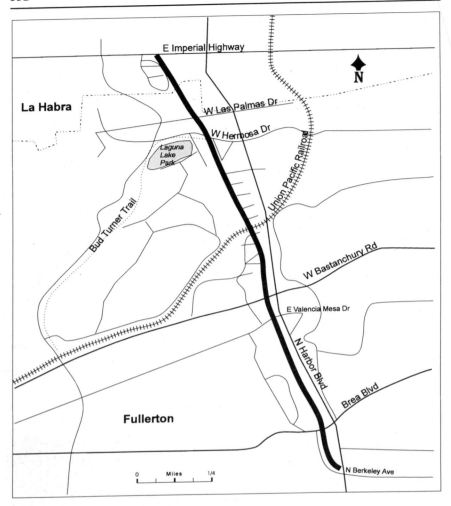

households. A narrow dirt path, used by both bicyclists and equestrians, parallels most of the trail. After crossing three roads it passes on an old trestle over the active Northern Pacific Railroad line.

When you get to West Hermosa Avenue you can go left (west) to Laguna Lake Park and enjoy its small pond. There are restrooms and picnic tables. The Bud Turner Trail passes by on the north side of the pond and continues west but it is not continuous or easy to follow.

To continue north on the trail, cross West Hermosa Avenue. From this point on the trail is unimproved with a dirt surface through a cut in the land. You will come out on the elevated dirt railroad. Where the grade ends, bear left along a narrow path between the canal and a fence. You will come out at East Imperial Highway in the city of La Habra.

44: WANDA ROAD PARK

Endpoints: East Katella Avenue to East Collins Avenue
Length: 0.5 mile
Surface: asphalt
Original Railroad: Santa Fe Railroad, abandoned 1977, trail built 1989
Restrictions: NMV
Location: Villa Park, Orange County
Manager: City of Villa Park

Directions: From State Highway 55, take the East Katella Avenue exit and head east. Turn right on Wanda Road. The trail starts at Wanda Road and East Katella Avenue and proceeds south.

(See map page 134.)

Description: Wanda Road Park is a winding pathway paralleling a minor arterial. It is a wonderful place for a short walk and heavily used by local residents for this purpose. The grass is kept trimmed and immaculate. To the right over a short wall is a residential neighborhood.

The railroad has been abandoned both north and south of this segment and there are plans to continue the trail in both directions as part of the Tustin Branch Trail. South it would connect with the Esplanade Trail, north and west it could connect with the Pacific Electric Bicycle Trail. Both of these trails are described elsewhere in this book.

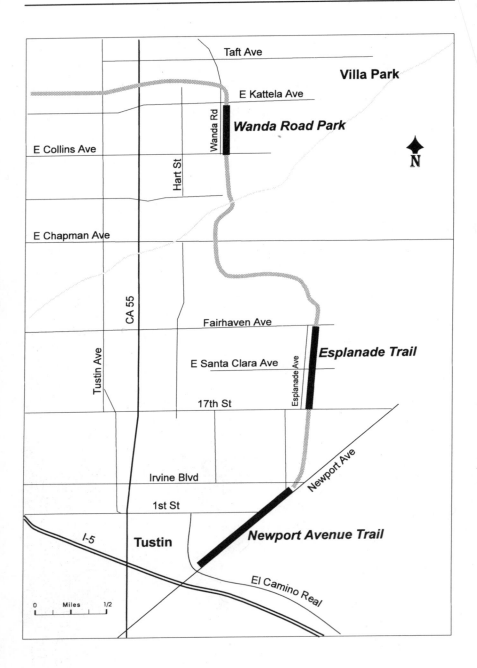

Taft Ave

Villa Park

E Kattela Ave

Wanda Rd

Wanda Road Park

E Collins Ave

Hart St

N

E Chapman Ave

CA 55

Fairhaven Ave

Tustin Ave

E Santa Clara Ave

Esplanade Ave

Esplanade Trail

17th St

Irvine Blvd

Newport Ave

1st St

I-5

Tustin

Newport Avenue Trail

El Camino Real

0   Miles   1/2

45: ESPLANADE TRAIL

Endpoints: Fairhaven Avenue to 17th Street
Length: 0.7 miles
Surface: dirt/gravel
Original Railroad: Santa Fe Railroad, abandoned 1969 and 1977
Restrictions: NMV
Location: North Tustin, Orange County
Manager: County of Orange

Directions: To get to the south end, from State Highway 55 take the 17th Street exit and head east three miles. Cross the trail at Esplanade Avenue. The trail travels north-south on the south side of Esplanade.

Description: The Esplanade Trail is a beautiful neighborhood rail-trail paralleling a minor arterial. It is a heavily landscaped strip and curves back and forth between bright purple and orange flowering plants. The trail has a dirt/gravel surface perfect for a stroll or a run as many local exercise walkers and joggers have found. There are picnic benches and water faucets along the entire route. With few other public parks nearby, the Esplanade Trail is one of the only open spaces available to the citizens of this un-incorporated part of the County of Orange.

South of 17th Street the railroad right-of-way is undeveloped for public use but you can see what a wide right-of-way was originally used by the railroad. The County of Orange has plans to connect the Esplanade Trail south to the Newport Avenue Trail and north to the Wanda Road Park. All three segments are part of the proposed Tustin Branch Trail which would go from Tustin to Orange for a distance of 6.5 miles and connect with the San Andreas Trail.

46: NEWPORT AVENUE TRAIL

Endpoints: Irvine Boulevard to El Camino Real
Length: 1 mile
Surface: asphalt
Original Railroad: Santa Fe Railroad, abandoned 1969 and 1977
Restrictions: NMV
Location: Tustin, Orange County
Manager: City of Tustin

Directions: From Interstate 5 take the Newport Avenue exit and head north. The trail begins on the north side of El Camino Real.

(See map page 134.)

Description: The Newport Avenue Trail is a narrow strip of land rescued from the heavy development in the center of Tustin. When the railroad was abandoned in 1977, Newport Avenue was widened using some of the railroad right-of-way. Fortunately, a thin sliver of land was preserved for non-motorized use. It is located along the edge of busy Newport Avenue, the main road through town and provides a safe place for bicyclists and walkers to traverse this very urban community. As part of the Tustin Branch Trail project there are plans to connect this trail north with the Esplanade Trail and the Wanda Road Park.

The trail is only eight feet wide and separated from Newport Avenue by a narrow planting strip or pavers. Despite its narrow width, it does provide some separation from motor vehicles. Although designed to accommodate bicycles, it is narrow and the frequent driveways make bicycle use dangerous. Use caution and do not expect car drivers to see you. Often they pull across the trail in order to see oncoming traffic.

With the further development of the Tustin Branch Trail, residents of Tustin and neighboring communities will have comparatively safe and unobstructed routes through town, thanks to the old railroad.

47: PACIFIC ELECTRIC BICYCLE TRAIL

Endpoints: East Chestnut Avenue to East Adams Avenue
Length: 2.1 miles
Surface: asphalt
Original Railroad: Pacific Electric Railroad Company, built 1920's
Restrictions: NMV
Location: Santa Ana, Orange County
Manager: City of Santa Ana

Directions: From Interstate 5, take the Fourth Street exit and head west two miles to the center of Santa Ana. Turn left on Garfield, right on 1st Avenue, and left on Maple. You will see railroad tracks still in the road. The rail-trail begins just south of East Chestnut Avenue.

Description: The Pacific Electric Bicycle Trail passes through a quiet residential area of Santa Ana. It is an example of how a long abandoned line naturally served as a quiet neighborhood park and bike route through a residential area and only after years of use was improved and officially designated a "trail." It follows the route of the original Red Car Line, a trolley system that ran throughout Los Angeles.

The trail starts near the center of Santa Ana and runs right down the middle of Maple Street. Maple Street then jogs and the trail continues to parallel it, wandering along a grass covered area between residential backyards. At 0.6 miles both the trail and Maple Street cross East

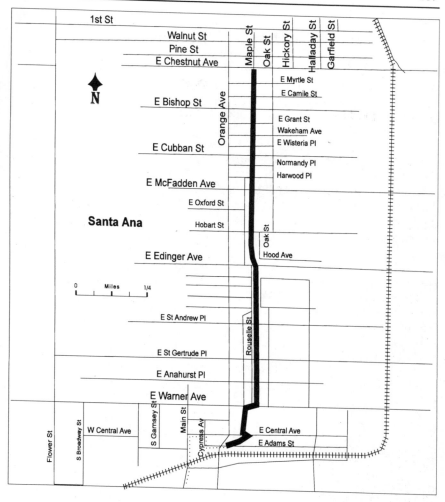

McFadden Avenue where the right-of-way becomes wider and the trail separates from Maple Street and meanders rather than going straight.

After first crossing East Edinger Avenue the trail narrows and parallels Maple and then Rouselle Streets. After crossing East Warner Avenue, it becomes a narrow path alongside a school and then continues south until it meets the active railroad line at Adams.

To connect with the Alton Bike Trail, turn right on Adams Street one block, right on Cypress one block, and left on East Central one block. Turn left on Main Street, right on Dyer Road and left on Flower Street. Look for the Alton Bike Trail on your right, parallel to the active line. The city of Santa Ana has plans to make a rail-trail connection from the Pacific Electric Bicycle Trail to the Alton Bike Trail in the future.

48: ALTON BIKE TRAIL

Endpoints: South Flower Street to Susan Street
Length: 1.8 miles
Surface: asphalt
Original Railroad: Southern Pacific Railroad (active)
Restrictions: NMV
Location: Santa Ana, Orange County
Manager: City of Santa Ana

Directions: From Interstate 405, take the South Bristol Street exit in Santa Ana. Head north one mile to Alton Avenue. Turn right and park on the street. The Alton Bike Trail parallels Alton Avenue going west and curves northeast alongside the active railroad.

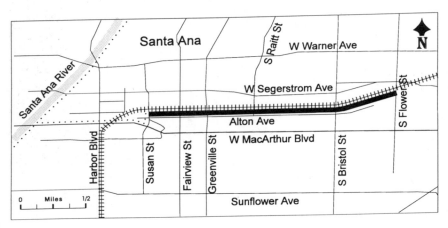

Description: The Alton Bike Trail is a popular commuter route and one of the few off-street bike paths in this heavily car-oriented city. It is also another good example of a trail sharing the same corridor with an active railroad.

The trail begins on South Flower Street adjacent to Saddleback High School. The path provides a safe route to and from school for many children. It heads west paralleling the Southern Pacific tracks, separated by a short cyclone fence which is enclosed with brush and trees. At Bristol Street the trail begins to parallel Alton Avenue going west. Here there is no physical barrier from the tracks which are about twenty feet north of the rail-trail.

The rail-trail continues west separated from Alton Avenue by two-foot wide stone pavers and ends at Susan Street. To continue west from there, turn left (south) on Susan Street one block to MacArthur Boulevard, a main arterial. Turn right and follow another separated path on the north side of MacArthur Boulevard. You can either stay on the path and pass over the Santa Ana River or drop down to the bike path on the east side of the river.

If you want to explore another rail-trail in one trip, you can continue east and connect with the Pacific Electric Bicycle Trail. From South Flower Street go north and turn right (east) on Dyer Road, left on Main Street, and right on Central Avenue. In two and a half blocks you will see the Pacific Electric Bicycle Trail crossing Central Avenue. The City of Santa Ana is considering extending the Alton Bike Trail alongside the existing railroad line so that the off-street connection is completed between it and the Pacific Electric Bicycle Trail.

49: HOOVER STREET BICYCLE TRAIL

Endpoints: Bolsa Avenue to Garden Grove Boulevard
Length: 2 miles
Surface: asphalt
Original Railroad: Southern Pacific Railroad
Restrictions: NMV
Location: Westminster, Orange County
Manager: City of Westminster

Directions: To get to the south end, from Interstate 405 in Westminster take the Bolsa Avenue exit and head east for almost a mile. The trail begins at the intersection of Hoover Street and Bolsa Avenue. To get to the north end, continue up Hoover Street for two miles to the corner of Garden Grove Boulevard and Hoover Avenue.

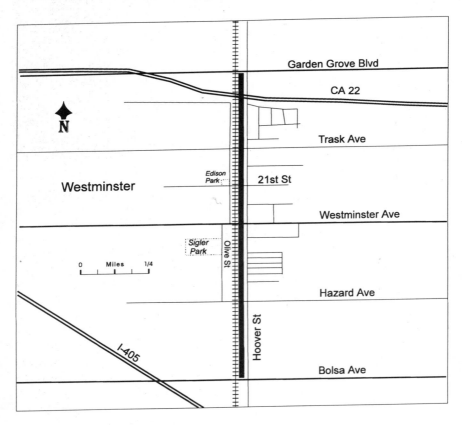

Description: The Hoover Street Bicycle Trail is constructed alongside an active railroad line and close to a busy street. Although not very scenic, it does provide a wide place to walk and a safe place for bicycling through Westminster.

Hoover Street is a four lane arterial in an industrial area. It does not have a sidewalk on either side. The railroad is an industrial spur with infrequent use and slow trains. The trail is forty feet from the rails, separated by a thick hedge south of Westminster Avenue. Just west of Hoover Street along Westminster Avenue is a small park, Sigler Park, which is a good place for those looking for shade to stop and take a rest.

This trail is not heavily used, probably because of its close proximity to Hoover Street, the absence of destinations at either end, and the lack of other easy non-motorized access or separated facilities. Landscaping would make it more attractive. Hoover Street ends going south at Bolsa Avenue, however, the railroad continues and it would be possible to continue the trail south also. With active citizen involvement the Hoover Street Bicycle Trail could be greatly improved and better utilized.

50: AT&SF BICYCLE TRAIL

Endpoints: Harvard Avenue to Sand Canyon Avenue
Length: 2.5 miles
Surface: asphalt
Original Railroad: Atchison Topeka and Santa Fe (AT&SF) Railroad Company (active), trail built 1977
Restrictions: NMV
Location: Irvine, Orange County
Manager: City of Irvine

Directions: To get to the southeast end, from Interstate 5 take the Sand Canyon Road exit and turn south. The trail starts on your right immediately after crossing over the railroad tracks. To get to the west end, from Interstate 5 take the Culver Road exit in Irvine and head southwest. In one half mile turn right on Walnut Avenue and in 3/4 mile left on Harvard Avenue. You will cross the railroad tracks and the trail in 1/2 mile.

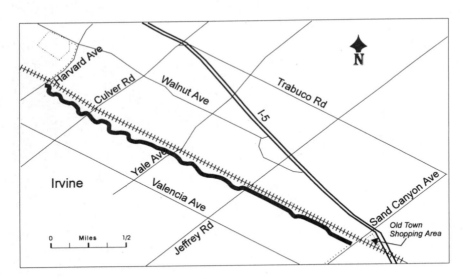

Description: The Atchison Topeka and Santa Fe (AT&SF) Bicycle Trail is another excellent example of a trail alongside an active working railroad. In this case, the railroad operates at the highest speeds of any in the state, up to 90 miles per hour. Southern California Edison owns the corridor along which the trail runs and uses it for its high

voltage lines. Because the corridor is so wide, it provides a safe place to walk or bicycle across Irvine away from the busy roads.

The best place to start is from the Harvard Community Athletic Park at the corner of Harvard Avenue and Walnut Avenue. Here you will find parking, restrooms, and playfields. Take the separated paved path on the north side of Harvard Avenue southwest until you come to the railroad tracks. The AT&SF Bicycle Trail starts on the southwest side of Harvard on the south side of the tracks. If you continue south on Harvard Avenue you can connect to the San Diego Creek Bike Trail.

The trail uses the Southern California Edison high voltage transmission right-of-way. The right-of-way is wide and the transmission towers are very tall so that you really are not aware of their presence. The trail meanders in big wide curves back and forth within the right-of-way making the trail longer. From Harvard Avenue to Culver Road the land is covered with grass and is bordered by a walled residential neighborhood to the southwest.

At Culver Road the trail crosses at the same grade as the road surface. Use caution in making this road crossing as Culver Road has busy, high-speed traffic. The City of Irvine is considering construction of an overpass over Culver Road for the trail.

From Culver Road to Yale Avenue the right-of-way is heavily landscaped with lush grass and small trees through which the trail wanders. There is a residential development on the southwest edge and a clear view of the passing trains to the northeast. Yale Avenue has an overpass for cars and there is access from both sides of the road to the trail. You can also stay on the trail and go directly under Yale Avenue.

Continuing southeast of Yale Avenue, the power line right-of-way is separated from the railroad right-of-way by a row of tall deciduous trees. This makes a beautiful visual buffer, unless you prefer to watch the the fastest trains in the state operate on the adjacent tracks.

At Jeffrey Road the trail crosses at grade. Southwest from here the trail runs straight next to a row of tall trees with views of orchards on the southeast side.

The trail ends at Sand Canyon Avenue. There is a separate path going southwest from this point to Irvine Center Road. Across Sand Canyon Avenue to the northeast is Old Town Irvine, a commercial area which includes an old fruit packing plant which has been converted to shops and restaurants.

51: ELECTRIC AVENUE GREENBELT MEDIAN PARK

Endpoints: Marina Drive to Seal Way
Length: 0.5 miles
Surface: concrete
Original Railroad: The Red Line
Restrictions: NMV, no horses
Location: Seal Beach, Orange County
Manager: City of Seal Beach

Directions: From Interstate 405, take the Seal Beach Boulevard exit and go south. Turn right and follow Seal Beach Boulevard. At the Pacific Coast Highway (State Highway 1) turn right. Turn left on Main Street and you will cross the rail-trail greenbelt. The old railroad grade ran down the middle of what is now Electric Avenue.

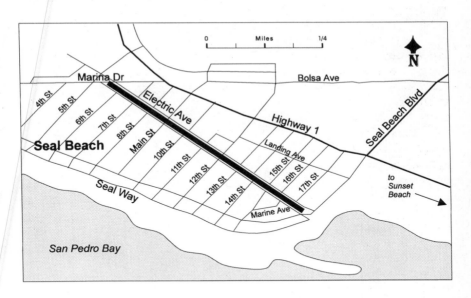

Description: The Electric Avenue Greenbelt Median Park is a beautiful trail built on a heavily landscaped parkway through the middle of the small beach community of Seal Beach. It is a wonderful place to go for a walk amidst large trees and manicured lawn. Although it is also open to bicycles, it was not designed for their use. The paths are narrow and better suited to walkers and/or children just learning to ride a bicycle. For experienced cyclists, the quiet streets of Seal Beach offer a more pleasant and varied place to ride.

At the north end is one of the old Red Line trolleys. These trolleys used to operate extensively throughout Los Angeles before cars took over. There are some plans to try and continue this trail south for another mile to Sunset Beach which would create a nice long walking route. At Sunset Beach you will find an old water tower used by the railroad that has been converted into a residence.

52: HERMOSA VALLEY GREENBELT

Endpoints:	Rosecrans Avenue to Ripley Avenue
Length:	3.7 miles
Surface:	wood chips
Original Railroad:	Atchison Topeka & Santa Fe Railroad, abandoned 1983, trail opened 1989
Restrictions:	NMV, no horses, not suitable for bicycles
Location:	Hermosa Beach, Manhattan Beach, Los Angeles County
Manager:	City of Hermosa Beach, City of Manhattan Beach

Directions: From Interstate 405, take the Manhattan Beach/ Rosecrans Avenue exit and turn west. Immediately after passing Valley Drive turn left into a large parking area. The trail begins at the south end of the parking area. To get to the south end, take the Redondo Beach/ Ripley Avenue exit from Interstate 405. Go west and access the trail at an unpaved parking area just before Valley Drive. There is no identified parking at this location.

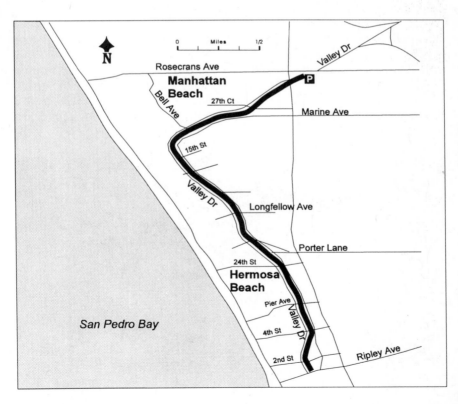

Description: The Hermosa Valley Greenbelt is the conversion of a railroad right-of-way which runs down the gentle Hermosa Valley between the communities of Hermosa Beach and Manhattan Beach. The surface is covered with bark chips and other chipped material from both cities' continuous tree pruning programs. This produces a soft walking and running surface in an area monopolized by cars. The greenway serves as a linear park used mostly by local citizens. It passes close to both central business districts and city halls.

Care should be taken when crossing the road intersections. Signs on the trail clearly indicate that cars have the right-of-way and that trail users must use the crosswalks and wait for the crossing lights. This "request" is emphasized by having high curbs where the trail intersects the roads and no trail-crossing signs. It is best recommended for a walk or running, definitely not for bicycling.

The trail begins at a parking lot in Manhattan Beach. In 0.4 miles it crosses 27th Court. At 1.2 miles it crosses 15th Street at an unusual and potentially dangerous intersection for trail users, so use the crosswalks and caution. At 1.4 miles cross Manhattan Beach Boulevard, again using the crosswalks. At 2.2 cross Gould Street. Note the sign which makes it clear that the cars have the right-of-way! To the west is the Theodore Pain Native Floral Area and a large park with play fields and restrooms. At this point on the trail a Par Course also begins. A parallel hard packed sand path parallels the trail in the City of Hermosa Beach. The trail ends at 3.7 miles at the southern boundary of Hermosa Beach.

This project was created when the citizens of Hermosa Beach chose to tax themselves and the Manhattan Beach City Council chose to participate in order to purchase this prime piece of real estate. It is now a beautiful green park that connects these two communities together and provides unique recreational opportunities for everyone.

53: *FAYE AVENUE BIKE PATH*

Endpoints: Faye Avenue to Via Del Norte
Length: 0.75 miles
Surface: asphalt
Original Railroad: San Diego, Pacific Beach, and La Jolla Railroad, built 1910
Restrictions: NMV
Location: La Jolla, San Diego County
Manager: City of San Diego, San Diego County

Directions: From Interstate 5, take the Ardath Road exit to La Jolla. Keep left as this becomes Torrey Pines Road. Turn right on Prospect Street and left on Faye Avenue. The path begins to the south of Nautilus Street.

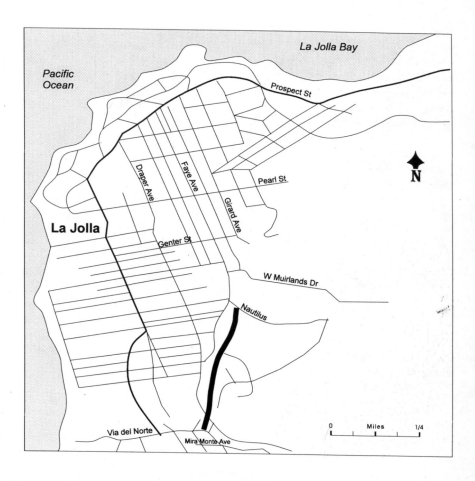

Description: The Faye Avenue Bike Path starts at the north just off of Faye Avenue and heads south. It is a quiet trail uphill and parallel to the busy main street that runs through the center of La Jolla. Slightly elevated above the main part of town, it provides occasional views out towards the ocean. Green grassy slopes that abut the trail offer one of the few publicly accessible green areas in La Jolla. Half way along the trail is a little park with picnic tables and a view to the west.

The path is paved south to Via del Norte making it ideal for most recreational activities. The land on either side has been left fairly natural and creates pleasant surroundings. Both these features have combined to make the Faye Avenue Bike Path a popular place for local residents to take walks, walk dogs, run, or ride bicycles.

54: ROSE CANYON BIKE PATH

Endpoints: Santa Fe Street to Regents Road
Length: 1.25 miles
Surface: asphalt
Original Railroad: Southern Pacific Railroad (active line), built 1913
Restrictions: NMV
Location: San Diego, San Diego County
Manager: City of San Diego

Directions: To get to the south end, from Interstate 5 in San Diego take the Balboa Avenue exit #274. Turn left under the freeway on Garnet Street. Turn left again on Damon Avenue and left again on Santa Fe Street, a frontage road which runs parallel to the freeway going north. Follow Santa Fe Street for two miles until you come to a turn around and the start of the trail. To get to the north end, from Interstate 5 take the La

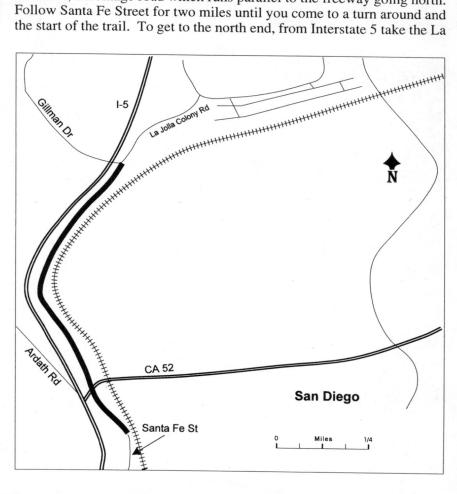

Jolla Colony exit and go north (left) on Gillman Drive. Take the first left into the park and ride lot and park there. The trail starts on the east side of Interstate 5 just south of this parking lot and goes downhill southbound.

Description: The Rose Canyon Bike Path is an important bypass route for bicyclists. When Interstate 5 was put in through this canyon, it obliterated the northern end of Santa Fe Street and cut off one of the few side roads going north from San Diego. The rail-trail parallels the active railroad and is down in a canyon below the freeway. It is a pleasant change for bicyclists from the busy and steep roads all around and makes possible a reasonable north-south route through this part of San Diego.

There are plans to continue this rail-trail up the coast for a total of 32 miles alongside the railroad. Such a long-distance route beside an active railroad would not only demonstrate the benefits railroad grades provide for non-motorized use in rugged country, it would provide overwhelming evidence of the compatibility of trails with active railway lines.

55: *SILVER STRAND BIKEWAY*

Endpoints:	Coronado to Imperial Beach
Length:	9 miles
Surface:	asphalt
Original Railroad:	San Diego and Arizona Railway, built 1907, abandoned 1951, trail built 1979-1981
Restrictions:	NMV, no horses
Location:	Coronado, San Diego County
Manager:	City of Coronado

Directions: To get to the north end, from Interstate 5 take the 1st Avenue exit and go south on 1st Avenue. Turn right on West Broadway and follow it west to the dock. From here you can take the San

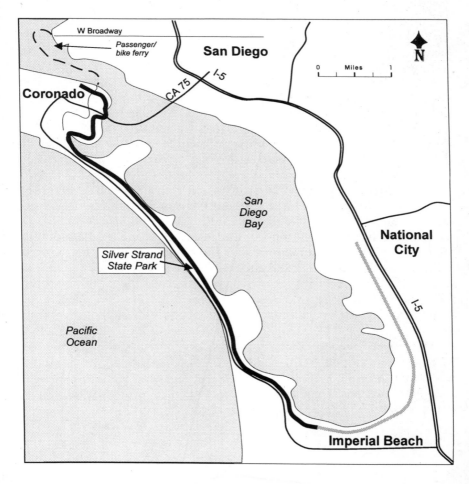

Diego passenger/bike ferry to Coronado (233-6872) where the rail-trail starts at the ferry terminal. Alternatively, from Interstate 5 take the State Highway 75 exit to Coronado, crossing a very high bridge over the San Diego Bay. Turn right on Orange Avenue and right on 1st. The trail starts at the ferry terminal as mentioned above. To get to the south end, from Interstate 5 going south take the State Highway 75 exit south of Chula Vista and head west to Imperial Beach. Turn right on 7th Street and go to the end of the road. The trail starts on your left.

Description: The Silver Strand Bikeway was constructed on the site of the old railroad grade which runs on the narrow spit of sand out to the community of Coronado. It provides a perfectly flat place to ride with views across the bay to San Diego. Because the railroad was built on the bay side of the spit you cannot see the ocean. At the south end the trail veers away from the noisy highway and is close to the wetlands at the edge of the bay.

At the northern terminus, the trail starts at the passenger/bike ferry in Coronado called the Landing, located at the foot of B Avenue, off First Street. Take the 10 minute ferry trip from the Broadway Pier in San Diego to get there or drive over on State Highway 75. The trail goes south and winds underneath the State Highway 75 bridge over San Diego Bay. It skirts a golf course and connects to Glorietta Boulevard. In one mile the trail passes by the Naval Amphibious base. In two miles you will pass Fiddler's Cove access road. In five miles you will come to the Silver Strand State Park with beach access. There is an underpass under the busy State Highway 75. There is also bus service with buses that have bicycle racks.

Continuing south from the state park there is almost no development until the spit turns inland. The south terminus of the trail is at Boulevard Avenue and 7th Street in Imperial Beach. For bicyclists who wish to continue south, turn right on 7th Street and go south to the highway. There are plans to continue this trail south and east along the bay and north along the bay back into San Diego.

APPENDICES

Appendix 1: Trail Managers

Conditions change with rail-trails. Rules change, sections may be closed, or new sections may be opened. We recommend that you contact the trail manager of any trail that you plan to visit to obtain the most up-to-date information. Appendix 1 alphabetically lists the trails in the book and gives the name of the trail manager and managing agency for each.

Appendix 2: Future Rail-Trails

There are several rail-trails which are being built at the time this book is being written. There are also a large number of additional projects which are being planned. Finally, there are an additional number of potential rail-trail projects which need to be planned. Appendix 2 contains these future trails listed by county and divided between those planned and those which are not yet planned but have a great potential.

Appendix 3: Railroad Abandonments

As a reference tool, we have included a list of abandonments which have gone through the ICC abandonment process. Some of these segments have been purchased by a short line railroad and are still active railroads. Some are rail-trails. But many existing abandonments are opportunities for rail-trails that await your exploration and support.

APPENDIX 1: TRAIL MANAGERS

Alton Bike Trail, 48

Paul Johnson   (714) 571-4211
Senior Parks Superintendent
Parks Department
405 West 5th St., Santa Ana, CA 92702

Atchison Topeka and Santa Fe Trail, 50

Pete Kolibaba   (714) 724-7350
Transportation Department
City of Irvine
1 Civic Center Plaza
P.O. Box 19575, Irvine, CA 92713

Sherri Miller   (714) 834-3137
County of Orange
300 N. Flower St., 7th Floor
P.O. Box 4048, Santa Ana, CA 92702-4048

Bizz Johnson Trail, 35

Stan Bales   (916) 257-0456
Bureau of Land Management
Eagle Lake Resource Area
705 Hall St., Susanville, CA 96130

Lassen National Forest   (916) 257-2151
Eagle Lake Ranger District
55 S. Sacramento St., Susanville, CA 96130

Black Diamond Mine Trail, 22

Steve Fiala   (510) 635-0135, ext. 2602
East Bay Regional Park District
2950 Peralta Oaks Ct.
P.O. Box 5381, Oakland, CA 94605-0381

Bol Park Bike Path, 15

Gayle Likens   (415) 329-2136
Transportation Division
City of Palo Alto
250 Hamilton Ave.
P.O. Box 10250, Palo Alto, CA 94303

Chico Bike Path, 34

Mike Parks   (916) 895-4951
Public Works Maintenance Supervisor
General Services Department
City of Chico
901 Fir St.
P.O. Box 3420, Chico, CA 95927

Creek Trail, 17

Dennis Mulgannon   (408) 259-5477
Park Ranger
Alum Rock Park
City of San Jose
16240 Alum Rock Ave., San Jose, CA 95127

Duarte Bike Trail, 42

Donna Mitzel   (818) 357-7931
City of Duarte
1600 Hunnington Drive, Duarte, CA 91010

East West Trail Link, 5

Ben Burto   (415) 927-5064
City of Corte Madera
300 Tamalpais Dr., Corte Madera, CA 94925

Electric Avenue Greenbelt Median Park, 51

Barry Curtis   (310) 431-2527
Planning Assistant
City of Seal Beach
Engineering/Public Works Department
211 8th Street, Seal Beach, CA 90740

Esplanade Trail, 45

Sherri Miller   (714) 834-3137
County of Orange
300 N. Flower St. 7th Floor
P.O. Box 4048, Santa Ana, CA 92702-4048

El Dorado County Trail, 29

Craven Alcott   (916) 621-5353
Parks Director
El Dorado County Parks Department
3000 Fairlane Ct., Suite 1, Placerville, CA 95667

Fairfield Linear Park, 23

Gretchen Stranzl McCann   (707) 428-7431
City of Fairfield
Fairfield Community Services Department
1000 Webster St., Fairfield, CA 94533

Faye Avenue Bike Path, 53

Michael E. Jackson   (619) 533-3110
Bicycle Coordinator
City of San Diego
1222 First Ave., M.S. 503, San Diego, CA 92101

Fillmore Trail, 40

Tony Perez   (805) 524-3701
City of Fillmore
524 Sespe Avenue, Fillmore, CA 93015

Hammond Trail, 37

Karen Suiker   (707) 445-7650
Business and Parks Manager
Humbolt County Parks Division
1106 Second St., Eureka, CA   95501

Hermosa Valley Greenbelt, 52

Hermosa Valley Greenbelt
Mary Rooney   (310) 318-0280
City of Hermosa Beach
710 Pier Avenue, Hermosa Beach, CA 90254

Manhattan Beach Parkway
James W. Wolfe   (310) 545-5621
Director of Parks and Recreation
City Hall
1400 Highland Avenue, Manhattan Beach, CA 90266

Hoover Street Bicycle Trail, 49

Peter Macktrang   (714) 898-3311 ext. 217
City Traffic Engineer
City of Westminster
8200 Westminster Boulevard, Westminster, CA 92683

Joe Rodota Trail, 10

Mickey Karagan   (707) 527-2041
Sonoma County Regional Parks Department
2300 County Center Suite 120A, Santa Rosa, CA 95403

Juanita Cooke Greenbelt, 43

Susan Hunt   (714) 738-6583
Community Services, Development Coordinator
City of Fullerton
303 West Commonwealth Avenue, Fullerton, CA 92632

Lafayette/Moraga Trail, 20

Steve Fiala   (510) 635-0135 ext. 2602
East Bay Regional Park District
2950 Peralta Oaks Ct.
P.O. Box 5381, Oakland, CA 94605-0381

Lands End Trail, 1

Steve Gazzano   (415) 556-8371
Ocean District Ranger
National Park Service
Golden Gate National Recreation Area,
Fort Mason, San Francisco, CA 94123

Larkspur Path, 4

Mark Miller   (415) 927-5110
City of Larkspur
400 Magnolia Ave., Larkspur, CA 94939

Levee Trail, 6

Ben Burto   (415) 927-5064
City of Corte Madera
300 Tamalpais Dr., Corte Madera, CA 94925

Loma Prieta Grade, 14

Forest of Nisene Marks State Park
Santa Cruz District   (408) 429-2850
California Parks Service
600 Ocean St., Santa Cruz, CA 95060

Los Gatos Creek Trail, 16

Michael LaRocca   (408) 354-6809
Los Gatos Parks Department
Town of Los Gatos
41 Miles Ave.
P.O. Box 949, Los Gatos, CA 95031

MacKerricher State Park, 38

Bill Perry   (707) 937-5804
District Supervisor
Russian River - Mendocino District
Highway 1, P.O. Box 440, Ft. Bragg, CA 95460

Merced River Trail, 25

Jim Eicher   (916) 985-4474
Department of Interior
Bureau of Land Management
63 Matoma St., Folsom, CA 95630

Midway Bike Path, 33

Mike Crump   (916) 538-7681
Director, Department of Public Works
Butte County
Oroville, CA 95965

Mill Valley-Sausalito Path, 3

Steve Petterle   (415) 499-6387
Marin County Dept. of Parks, Open Space & Cultural Services
Marin Civic Center, Room 417
3501 Civic Center Dr., San Rafael, CA 94903

Monterey Bay Coastal Trail, 13

Monterey Section
Doug Stafford   (408) 646-3860
Parks Superintendent
City of Monterey
23 Ryan Ranch Rd., Monterey, CA 93940

Pacific Grove Section
John Miller, Director   (408) 372-2809
Pacific Grove Recreation Department
515 Gunipero Ave., Pacific Grove, CA 93950

Seaside Section
Parks Division   (408) 899-6236
440 Hardcort Ave., City of Seaside, CA 93955

Mt. Lowe Truck Trail, 41

Don Gilliland   (818) 790-1151
District Ranger
Arroyo-Seco Ranger District, U.S. Forest Service
Oak Grove Park, Flintridge, CA 91011

Newport Avenue Trail, 46

Sherri Miller   (714) 834-3137
County of Orange
300 N. Flower St. 7th Floor
P.O. Box 4048, Santa Ana, CA 92702-4048

Ojai Valley Trail, 39

Andrew Oshita   (805) 654-3945
Parks Manager
Ventura County Parks
800 South Victoria, Ventura, CA 93009

Old Railroad Grade, 2

Robert Badarocco   (415) 924-4600 ext. 294
Lands Division Manager
Marin Municipal Water District
220 Nellen Avenue, Corte Madera, CA 94925

Pacific Electric Bicycle Trail, 47
Paul Johnson   (714) 571-4211
Senior Parks Superintendent
Parks Department
City of Santa Ana
405 West 5th St., M-23, Santa Ana, CA 92702

Paradise Memorial Trailway, 32
Al McGreehan   (916) 872-6284
Community Development Director
Community Development Department
Town of Paradise
5555 Skyway, Paradise, CA 95969

Rose Canyon Bike Trail, 54
Michael E. Jackson   (619) 533-3110
Bicycle Coordinator
City of San Diego
1222 First Ave., M.S. 503, San Diego, CA 92101

Sacramento Northern Bike Trail, 24
Mike Matsuoka   (916) 264-5326
Landscape Architecture
City of Sacramento
1023 J St., Sacramento, CA 95814

Sacramento River Trail, 36
Terry Hanson   (916) 225-4095
City of Redding Parks and Recreation
760 Parkview Avenue, Redding, CA 96001-3396

San Ramon Valley Iron Horse Trail, 21
Steve Fiala   (510) 635-0135 ext. 2602
East Bay Regional Park District
2950 Peralta Oaks Ct.
P.O. Box 5381, Oakland, CA 94605-0381

Santa Fe Greenway, 18

El Cerrito Section
Beth Bartke   (510) 215-4382
Management Assistant
Maintenance and Engineering Services Division
City of El Cerrito
10890 San Pablo Ave., El Cerrito CA 94530

Albany Section
Jason Baker   (510) 528-5759
Engineering Assistant
Community Development and Environmental Resource Dept.
1000 San Pablo Ave., Albany, CA 94706

Berkeley Section
Jimmie Lee   (510) 644-6566
Senior Landscape Gardener Supervisor
City of Berkeley
1325 Bancroft Way, Berkeley, CA 94702

Shepherd Canyon Bike Trail, 19

Martin Matarrese   (510) 482-7849
Parkland Resources Supervisor
City of Oakland
1520 Lakeside Dr., Oakland, CA 94612

Silver Strand Bikeway, 55

Alan Williams   (619) 522-7380
Public Services Department
1300 1st St., Coronado, CA 92118

Sir Francis Drake Bikeway, 8

Shafter Bridge to Jewell
Lanny Waggoner   (415) 488-9897
State Park Ranger
Samuel P. Taylor State Park
P.O. Box 251, Lagunitas, CA 94938

Jewell to Tocaloma
Superintendent   (415) 663-8522
Pt. Reyes National Seashore
Pt. Reyes, CA 94956

Sonoma Bike Path, 12

Patricia Wagner   (707) 938-3743
City of Sonoma
#1 The Plaza, Sonoma, CA 95476

Sugarpine Railway Trail, 28

Beth Chacon   (209) 586-3234
Mi-Wuk Ranger District
U.S. Forest Service
Mi-Wuk Village
P.O. Box 100, CA 95346

Tiburon Lineal Park, 7

Tony Iacopi   (415) 435-7399
Department of Public Works
City of Tiburon
1175 Tiburon Boulevard, Tiburon, CA 94920

Tomales Bay Rail-Trail, 9

Tomales Bay State Park
Carlos Porrata   (415) 669-1140
Inverness, CA 94937

Pt. Reyes National Seashore
Supervisor   (415) 663-8522
Pt. Reyes National Seashore
Pt. Reyes, CA 94956

Truckee River Bike Trail, 31

Sandy Coambs, Director   (916) 583-5544
Tahoe City Department of Parks and Recreation
Tahoe City P.U.D.
P.O. Box 33, Tahoe City, CA 95730

Wanda Road Park, 44

Fred Mailey   (714) 998-1500
City of Villa Park
17855 Santiago Boulevard, Villa Park, CA 92667

West County Trail, 10

Mickey Karagan   (707) 527-2041
Sonoma County Regional Parks Department
2300 County Center, Suite 120A, Santa Rosa, CA 95403

West Side Railroad Trail, 27

Beth Chacon   (209) 586-3234
Mi-Wuk Ranger District
U.S. Forest Service
Mi-Wuk Village
P.O. Box 100, CA 95346

West Side Rails, 26

Beth Chacon   (209) 586-3234
Mi-Wuk Ranger District
U.S. Forest Service
Mi-Wuk Village
P.O. Box 100, CA 95346

Western States Pioneer Express Trail, 30

Rick LeFlore   (916) 988-0205
California Parks Service, American River District
7806 Folsom-Auburn Rd, Folsom, CA 95630

APPENDIX 2: FUTURE RAIL-TRAILS

PLANNED RAIL-TRAILS

In addition to the many rail-trails that are open in California, there are a number of new trails being planned. These trails have some public agency working on their creation and are in some stage of master planning, acquisition, or applying for funds. Some of these may actually be developed by the time you read this book. Check with the contacts listed below for more information or contact the county Parks Department. In many cases, these trails need your support and interest in order for them to become a reality.

Alameda and Contra Costa Counties

The East Bay Regional Park District has been a leader in the development of rail-trails in California. In addition to the three trails that they currently have open, they have plans for a number of extensions of these trails as well as new trails. Their jurisdiction includes both of these counties. A few of their projects are listed below.

Fremont to Pleasanton
Niles Canyon
Niles Canyon to Shadow Cliffs
Pleasanton to San Joaquin County Line
Pleasanton through Livermore to Tracy
Pleasanton to San Ramon
Alamo to Avon

For more information contact:
Steve Fiala   (510) 635-0135 ext. 2602
East Bay Regional Park District
2950 Peralta Oaks Ct.
P.O. Box 5381, Oakland, CA 94605-0381

El Dorado and Sacramento Counties

Folsom to Placerville
This would be an outstanding route leading from the Sacramento River Valley up into the mountains. This railroad line has been abandoned.

For more information contact:
Rick LeFlore   (916) 988-0205 ext. 23
California Parks Service, American River District
7806 Folsom-Auburn Road, Folsom, CA 95630

Craven Alcott   (916) 621-5353
Parks Director
El Dorado County Parks Department
3000 Fairlane Court, Suite 1, Placerville, CA 95667

Humbolt County

Little River Trail
For more information contact:
Karen Suiker   (707) 445-7650
Business and Parks Manager
Humbolt County Parks Division
1106 Second Street, Eureka, CA   95501

Don Beers   (707) 445-6547
Trinidad State Park
600A West Clark, Eureka, CA 95501

Los Angeles County

Burbank/Chandler Corridor
Santa Monica Boulevard
Exposition Boulevard
Pasadena Blue Line

For more information contact:
Cynthia D'Agosta   (213) 738-2973
Trails Coordinator/Planner
Los Angeles County
Department of Parks and Recreation
433 South Vermont Ave., Los Angeles, CA 90020-1975

Santa Clara River Trail

This is a proposed project to build a rail-trail from Santa Clarita to Ventura alongside the Santa Clara River, a distance of more than 50 miles. The Santa Clara River is the only major river that has not been channelized with concrete in the Los Angeles area and still retains much of its natural beauty. By 1996 a new section of this trail inside Santa Clarita will be developed starting at the MetroLink station in Santa Clarita and heading east.

For more information contact:
Joe Inch   (805) 286-4148
City of Santa Clarita
23920 Valencia Boulevard, Suite 120, Santa Clarita, CA 91355

Cross Marin Bike Trail

This is a major project to develop a bike route from Sausalito north following the former Northwestern Pacific Railroad right-of-way through Marin County.

For more information contact:
Steve Petterle   (415) 499-6387
Marin County Dept. of Parks, Open Space and Cultural Services
Marin Civic Center, Room 417
3501 Civic Center Dr., San Rafael, CA 94903

Marin County

San Rafael to Point San Quentin

Anderson Drive is going to be extended using part of the Northwestern Pacific Railroad's former right-of-way. A separated bike path will be constructed between Bellam Avenue and 2nd Street in downtown San Rafael.

For more information contact:
Steve Petterle   (415) 499-6387
Marin County Dept. of Parks, Open Space and Cultural Services
Marin Civic Center, Room 417
3501 Civic Center Dr., San Rafael, CA 94903

Tunnel Lane to Palm Avenue, City of Corte Madera

This short segment is being proposed for development in the City of Corte Madera along the Northwestern Pacific line. It will connect from an abandoned railroad tunnel north into the Larkspur Trail.

For more information contact:
Ben Burto   (415) 927-5064
City of Corte Madera
300 Tamalpais Dr., Corte Madera, CA 94925

Mono County

Bodie to Mono Lake Trail
This is a very scenic trail located on the east side of the Sierra Nevada. Bodie is an historic mining town and the trail winds down to Mono Lake.

For more information contact:
Charlie Willard   (916) 653-8803
California Parks Service
P.O. Box 942896
Sacramento, CA 94296-0001

Bureau of Land Management
Mono County

Monterey County

Pt. Lobos to Elkhorn Slough
This is a proposed extension of the Monterey Bay Coastal Trail both north and south. There is a long segment north of Sand City to Marinia which is already nearly complete.

For more information contact:
Gary Tate   (408) 659-4488
Monterey Peninsula Regional Park District
P.O. Box 935, Carmel Valley, CA 93924

Orange County

Rose Drive to Lemon Drive
Glassell Street to Fern Street
Collins Avenue to Chapman Avenue
Chapman Avenue to Fairhaven Avenue (at Esplanade Avenue)

17th Street to Plaza Way
Jeffrey Road to Edinger Avenue (including the Narrows)
Santa Ana to Garden Grove, Pacific Electric Railroad line
There are a number of rail-trail projects being planned in Orange County. Many of these will be placed alongside light rail lines.

For more information contact:
Sherri Miller   (714) 834-3137
County of Orange
300 N. Flower St. 7th Floor
P.O. Box 4048, Santa Ana, CA 92702-4048

Sacramento County

Sacramento to Locke
This project would follow a long-abandoned railroad line going south from Sacramento through farm land and would end at the small community of Locke.

Sacramento to Folsom
This project would connect Sacramento to Folsom Lake via the former Sacramento Northern Railroad line.

San Diego County

Coastal Bike Path
This would be an extension of the Rose Canyon Bike Path 35 miles north to Ocean Side. A preliminary engineering study has been conducted with the trail paralleling the active main line railroad.

For more information contact:
Steve Jantz   (619) 438-1161 ext. 4354
Community Development Services
Engineering Section
2075 Las Palmas Dr.
San Diego, CA 92009

North Country Trail, Oceanside to Escondido
This abandoned railroad corridor is being converted to light rail and there is a proposal to build a trail alongside the 12 miles of corridor which runs parallel to State Highway 78.

For more information contact:
    Steve Jantz   (619) 438-1161 ext. 4354
    Community Development Services
    Engineering Section
    2075 Las Palmas Dr.
    San Diego, CA 92009

Bayshore Bikeway

This project would be a continuation of the Silver Strand Bikeway through Imperial Beach and north up the east side of San Diego Bay adjacent to existing railroad right-of-way.

For more information contact:
    Michael E. Jackson   (619) 533-3110
    Bicycle Coordinator
    City of San Diego
    1222 First Ave., M.S. 503, San Diego, CA 92101

San Mateo County

Embarcadero Trail

This is a proposed section of a trail being built alongside an active main line railroad. While only about 1/2 mile in length, it provides an important link through Palo Alto for walkers and bicyclists.

For more information contact:
    Gayle Likens   (415) 329-2136
    Transportation Division
    City of Palo Alto
    250 Hamilton Ave.
    P.O. Box 10250, Palo Alto, CA 94303

Ravenswood Drill

This is a proposed short section of trail built alongside an unused but not abandoned line.

For more information contact:
    Craig Britton   (415) 949-5500
    Midpeninsula Regional Open Space District
    Old Mill Office Center, Building C, Suite 135
    201 San Antonio Circle, Mountain View, CA 94040

Santa Barbara County

Sandpiper-Las Palmas
This project would construct a trail between these two small communities in Santa Barbara.

Carpinteria to Goleta
This project will develop a 15 mile trail alongside Southern Pacific Railroad tracks passing through Carpinteria and Goleta. It has been discussed for many years but needs public support to make it become a reality.

For more information contact:
  Wilson Hubbel   (805) 568-3000, ext. 3046

Santa Maria Valley Railroad Bikeway
This is a 2.5 mile abandoned line which goes from Main Street in Guadalupe to the airport. It will be opened in 1996.

For more information contact:
  Richard Sweet   (805) 925-0951, ext. 225
  City of Santa Maria
  Engineering Department
  705 West Cypress
  Santa Maria, CA 93454

Santa Clara County

Steven's Creek Rail-Trail, Mt. View, CA
Lick (north of Edenvale) to Alamitos

Siskiyou County

Yreka Creek Greenway
This project includes a segment of a bicycle path to be constructed adjacent to the Blue Goose scenic railroad.

For more information contact:
  Jerry Mosier   (916) 842-6131
  Yreka Creek Greenway Steering Committee
  c/o Klamath National Forest
  1312 Fairlane Road, Yreka, CA 96097

Shasta County

Redding to Old Shasta

The City of Redding is planning to construct a trail from Riverside Park to Old Shasta including an old railroad grade and stage road.

For more information contact:
Terry Hanson   (916) 225-4095
City of Redding Parks and Recreation
760 Parkview Avenue, Redding, CA 96001-3396

Old Shasta to Shasta Dam

This is a tremendous route which follows along the Sacramento River below Shasta Dam. This area is quite remote, in a deep gorge, and provides a spectacular setting for the trail.

For more information contact:
Steve Ulls or Eric Morgan   (916) 224-2100
Middle Creek Road, Redding, CA 96001

Solano County

Vacaville to east of Cordelia

This is a proposed route connecting the cities of Vacaville and Fairfield via the former Sacramento Northern Railroad right-of-way.

For more information contact:
Robert Farrington
City of Vacaville
650 Merchant Street, Vacaville, CA 95688

Fairfield-Suisun to Rio Vista Junction

This is a former Sacramento Northern line which ran from Suisan City near Fairfield to Rio Vista Junction.

For more information contact:
Gretchen Stranzl McCann   (707) 428-7431
City of Fairfield
Fairfield Community Services Department
1000 Webster Street, Fairfield, CA 94533

Sonoma County

Sebastopol to Forestville

This is a proposed extension of the West County Trail to the northwest. It would follow the Northwestern Pacific right-of-way for much of the route. Some of this right-of-way has been lost to development but much of it is still intact.

Sebastopol to Santa Rosa
This is a proposed extension east of the Joe Rodota Trail into downtown Santa Rosa at Roberts Avenue just west of State Highway 101 near Railroad Square.

Sebastopol to Petaluma
Petaluma to Donahue Landing

Sonoma to Agua Caliente
This is a proposed two mile extension of the Sonoma Bike Path. The continuation would start at the current west terminus at the Sonoma Regional Park and continue north to Agua Caliente.

Sonoma to Schellville
This is a proposed extension of the Sonoma Bike Path going south to a small crossroads called Schellville at the intersection of State Highways 12 and 121. This project needs support for funding.

For more information about Sonoma County rail-trails contact:
Micki Carrigan   (707) 527-2041
Sonoma County Regional Parks
County Complex, 410 Fiscal Dr., Santa Rosa, CA 95403

Ventura County

Ventura to Foster Park
This is a current acquisition project which would ultimately extend the Ojai Valley Trail into Ventura.

Ventura to Piru
This is part of a proposed rail-with-trail project following the Santa Ana River which would connect Ventura to Santa Clarita in Los Angeles County.

Limoneira Spur
This is a short railroad spur off of the Ventura to Piru route which is being purchased for future rail-with-trail use.

For more information contact:
Ron Blakemore   (805) 654-3962
Regional Trails and Pathways Program
County of Ventura
800 South Victoria Avenue, Ventura, CA 93009

POTENTIAL RAIL-TRAILS

All railroads are potential rail-trail prospects. Whether abandoned long ago or still active, they can all be converted to valuable recreational and non-motorized transportation facilities. For a complete listing of all abandonments in California, please turn to Appendix 3. The purpose of this section is to highlight some lines that have been abandoned and have not yet been targeted for development, but would make exceptional rail-trails. This should make it easier for readers to identify projects in their vicinity that they would like to champion or promote.

Abandoned Lines

Alameda County

7th Street Pier to Point View Park, City of Oakland

Alameda and Contra Costa Counties

Oakland to Moraga
This route would start at the waterfront of Oakland, ascend the Shepherd Canyon Trail, and return down the other side of the hills into Moraga. It will be difficult to build because much of the route has been destroyed by State Highway 13 and State Highway 24.

Butte County

Paradise to Sterling City, abandoned 1977

Inyo and Kern Counties

Searles to Lone Pine, 84 miles
Visalia Electric Line

Los Angeles County

Southern Pacific Santa Paula Branch
Southwest Long Beach Corridor

San Vincente Boulevard/Burton Way
Inglewood Branch
Normandie Avenue
Harbor Belt , San Pedro Belt , and Wilmington Harbor Lines
West Santa Ana Branch/Pacific Electric Line
Southern Pacific Whittier Branch
Huntington Drive
Chino Pomona Line
Venice Boulevard
Moorpark Metrolink
Santa Claria Metrolink/Southern Pacific Saugus Line
Norwalk El Segundo Green Line
Metropolitan Transportation Authority's Harbor Subdivision
Southern Pacific Hawthorne Branch
Del Amo Boulevard Railroad
Torrance Place Railroad
Long Beach Blue Line Light Rail Corridor
Union Pacific Corridor - South Long Beach
Azusa Spur
Pasadena — Sam Dimas Corridor
San Benardino Metrolink

Marin and Sonoma Counties

Novato to Healdsburg
This is part of the former Northwestern Pacific Railroad right-of-way and would extend north the Marin County Bike Path.

Glenellen to Schellville, Sonoma County
This is an extension of the Sonoma Bike Trail going south. It would also be possible to connect Schellville to Vineburg.

For more information contact:
Micki Carrigan   (707) 527-2041
Sonoma County Regional Parks
County Complex, 410 Fiscal Dr., Santa Rosa, CA 95403

Modoc and Siskiyou Counties

Chippy Spur to Lookout Junction
This is a 33 mile section of the Northern Pacific line near Habrone.

Orange County

City of Cypress to the City of Santa Ana
Seal Beach Boulevard to Phillips Road (at Surfside)
San Clemente Trail
Palm Street to Kraemer Boulevard
Fullerton Station to Orangethorpe Avenue
Los Alamitos Boulevard to Beach Boulevard
Bolsa Avenue to Garfield Avenue

Placer and Nevada Counties

High Sierra Rail-trail
This trail would follow the route of the original trans-continental railroad over the Sierras. The section between Truckee and Immigrant Gap, a distance of 25 miles, has had the rails and ties removed.

For more information contact:
Kathy Haggen-Smith   (916) 663-4626
Placer Bikeways and Trails Partnership
P.O. Box 6356
Auburn, CA 95604

San Francisco and San Mateo Counties

Daly City to Tunitas
The Coast Walkers, Trust for Public Land, and San Mateo Bikeway Advisory Committee all have expressed interest in this route. The biggest challenge is that much of the original right-of-way has been washed into the sea.

San Joaquin County

Lodi to Kentucky House

Santa Clara County

Los Gatos (Vasona Station) to Santa Cruz County
The Southern Pacific Railroad ran along Los Gatos creek from Vasona Station to Los Gatos along the west side of Lexington Reservoir and then through the Santa Cruz Mountains to Wrights, Laurel, and Santa Cruz. Two tunnels have been partially dynamited, in Wrights and Laurel, but many segments are still intact. There has been interest expressed in this route by Santa Cruz County and the City of San Jose.

Lick (north of Edenvale) to Alamitos
This project would be part of either State Highway 85 expansion or a light rail project. The corridor runs from State Highway 82 to McKean Road.

Ventura County

Piru to County Line
Santa Paula Branch
Port Hueneme Lines

Not Abandoned Yet

There is no easy way of predicting which railroads will decide to abandon sections of track. Those interested in rail-trails need to be prepared for any segment of track being abandoned at any time. If no other railroad steps forward to operate a railroad, an agency already needs to have filed for railbanking in order to preserve the corridor. Planning work needs to be done before the railroad files for abandonment.

We are **not** advocating that any of these lines be abandoned. However, if they are abandoned we would like for public officials and the public to be aware of their potential for rail-trail use. There is also the possibility for a trail alongside the rails on some of these routes. Potential segments include:

Castroville to Seaside, Monterey County
Likely to be developed as a passenger service line to Santa Cruz.

Oakdale to Standard, Stanislaus and Tuolumne Counties
This segment is not likely to be abandoned as it serves a major lumbermill, but would be a great route from the valley into the mountains. Keep watching in case the situation changes.

Willits to Fort Bragg, Mendocino County
This is currently a very popular tourist train route winding through the Redwoods.

Willits to Eureka, Mendocino and Humbolt Counties
This is a very long route which is important to the north coast, but very expensive to maintain as a railroad. If ever abandoned, it would make a great trail.

Napa to Krug, Napa County
There is potential for a trail alongside the existing railroad, the route of the Napa Valley Wine Train.

San Jose to Permente, San Mateo County
Oxnard to Lancaster, Los Angeles County
Searles to Trona, Kern, and San Bernadino Counties
San Diego to El Cajon, San Diego County
Mt. Shasta to Burnay, Shasta County
Weed to Hilt (Oregon Border), Siskiyou County
Ignacio to Sonoma, Sonoma County
Dougherty to Tadum

APPENDIX 3: RAILROAD ABANDONMENTS IN CALIFORNIA

County	Branch	Mileage	Date	Railroad
Alameda/San Joaquin	Niles	36.4	9/16/82	SPTCo
Alameda	Radum	5.7	8/12/85	SPTCo
Alameda	Main	0.6	12/13/85	AT&SF
Alameda	Main	1.5	2/18/86	WP
Alameda	Main	0.8	1/30/87	AT&SF
Alameda	Main	0.6		AT&SF
Butte/Yuba	Oroville	0.9	3/7/84	SPTCo
Butte	Stirling City	3.3	9/4/84	SPTCo
Butte/Yuba	Oroville	0.8	10/2/84	SPTCo
Colusa/San Joaquin	Kentucky House	31.8	3/14/84	SPTCo
Colusa	Colusa	4.1	10/12/84	SPTCo
Contra Costa/SF	Oakland District	10.4	9/9/85	AT&SF
Contra Costa	Avon	2.1	7/10/87	SPTCo
Contra Costa	Port Chicago	1.2	8/30/94	UP
El Dorado	Main	8.0	7/31/86	CaPlac& LkTahoe
El Dorado	Diamond Springs	4.9	6/18/90	SPTCo
Fresno/King	Laton	17.6	11/13/80	AT&SF
Fresno	Coalinga	2.6	1/18/83	SPTCo
Fresno	Exeter	3.6	7/11/83	SPTCo
Fresno	Coalinga	12.3	9/12/83	SPTCo
Fresno	Riverdale	2.2	9/16/83	SPTCo
Fresno	Wahtoke	4.2	5/25/84	AT&SF
Fresno	Biola	8.7	12/4/84	SPTCo
Fresno	FresnoInturbn	10.9	6/13/85	AT&SF
Fresno	Main	10.9	6/13/85	Fresno Intrurban
Fresno	Wahtoke	2.0	1/30/87	AT&SF
Fresno	Clovis	4.5	3/9/94	SPTCo
Fresno	Main	4.5	3/9/94	SJVTT
Fresno	Main	4.5	5/9/94	SJVTT
Fresno/Tulare	Main	58.8	9/26/94	TVRR
Fresno	Clovis	4.5		SPTCo
Fresno	Biola	8.7		SPTCo
Fresno	Coalinga	13.9		SPTCo
Fresno	Fresno Interurban	10.8	1/7/85	SPTCo

County	Branch	Mileage	Date	Railroad
Humbolt	Main	7.5	4/23/85	Arcadia &MadR
Humbolt	Main	98.0	5/15/85	NWP
Imperial		18.5	8/22/79	SPT/ SD&AE
Imperial	Main	10.5	10/31/85	Holton INtr/SPT
Imperial	Sandia	11.7	7/23/90	SPTCo
Kern/Inyo	Lone Pine	89.3	3/12/82	SPTCo
Kings/Tulare	Main	29.5	3/24/94	TVRR
Kings	Main	8.3	4/29/94	SJVTT
Lassen	Susanville	2.7	10/18/95	SPTCo
Los Angeles			3/23/81	GrPaC&n
Los Angeles	West Santa Ana	3.3	1/13/83	SPTCo
Los Angeles	Redondo Beach	4.6	4/12/83	AT&SF
Los Angeles	West Los Angeles	4.6	7/29/83	SPTCo
Los Angeles	West Santa Ana	0.0	6/20/84	SPTCo
Los Angeles	East Long Beach	5.2	4/4/85	SPTCo
Los Angeles	Pasadena	1.3	7/9/85	LA&SL
Los Angeles	Pasadena	1.3	7/9/85	UP
Los Angeles	Santa Monica	5.2	3/12/86	SPTCo
Los Angeles	Whittier	2.5	3/13/86	SPTCo
Los Angeles	Pasadena	2.1	9/27/88	AT&SF
Los Angeles	Glendale	1.3	7/3/89	UP
Los Angeles	Glendale	4.0	8/22/90	UP
Los Angeles	San Bernadino	15.5	5/6/92	SPTCo
Los Angeles	Santa Monica		5/6/92	SPTCo
Los Angeles/Orange	Baldwin Park	4.1	5/20/92	SPTCo
Los Angeles	Burbank	4.5	5/20/92	SPTCo
Los Angeles	Santa Monica	6.9	5/20/92	SPTCo
Los Angeles	Santa Paula	16.6	11/30/92	SPTCo
Los Angeles	Pasadena	16.0	2/14/94	AT&SF
Los Angeles	Pasadena	16.0	2/14/94	MTA
Los Angeles	Burbank	5.9	5/24/94	SPTCo
Los Angeles	Burbank	2.4	6/28/94	LACMTA
Los Angeles	Burbank	2.4	6/28/94	SPTCo
Los Angeles	Burbank	5.2	6/28/94	LACMTA
Los Angeles	Burbank	5.2	6/28/94	SPTCo
Los Angeles	State St/Burbank			SCRRA
Los Angeles				AT&SF
Los Angeles	San Pedro	1.8	8/10/87	SPTCo
Marin	San Rafael	1.4	7/13/82	NWP

County	Branch	Mileage	Date	Railroad
Marin	San Rafael	10.0	9/29/89	NWP
Marin	San Rafael	11.3		NWP
Marin	San Rafael	11.5		NWP
Mendocino		40.0	8/27/86	
Mendocino	Main	40.0		Cal West
Merced/Fresno	West Side Line	18.7	9/29/94	SPTCo
Modoc/Siskiyou	Lookout/Hambron	33.4		BN
Modoc/Siskiyou	Main	33.4		BN
Modoc	Lakeview	54.5		SPTCo
Napa	Napa	21.3	10/15/85	SPTCo
Orange	Tustin	1.8	12/11/81	SPTCo
Orange	Tustin	1.8	6/1/83	SPTCo
Orange	Anaheim	0.4	4/14/86	LA&SL
Orange	Anaheim	0.4	2/25/87	SPTCo
Orange	Anaheim	1.5	3/7/88	SPTCo
Orange	Anaheim	0.4		UP
Orange	Anaheim	0.7		UP
Orange		5.4		AT&SF
Riverside	Elsinore	18.5	9/11/81	AT&SF
Riverside	Main	1.4	9/9/82	UP
Riverside	San Jacinto	22.0		AT&SF
Sacramento	Swanston	1.3	2/25/82	SN
Sacramento	R Street	3.4	9/6/85	SPTCo
Sacramento	R Street	3.4	9/6/85	SPTCo
Sacramento	Walnut Grove	2.3	2/13/86	SPTCo
Sac/El Dorado	Placerville	37.1	10/31/94	SPTCo
San Bernadino	Redlands	6.5	11/30/80	AT&SF
San Bernadino	Redlands	3.3	6/21/85	SPTCo
San Bernadino	Redlands	2.0	11/14/94	AT&SF
San Bernadino	Redlands	2.0		SANBAG
San Bernadino	Redlands	4.0		AT&SF
San Diego	Main		8/29/79	Kyle
San Diego	Fallbrook	16.5	3/16/81	AT&SF
San Diego/Imperial	Main	55.2		RailTex
San Diego/Imperial		153.0		SD&IVRR
San Fran/Santa Clara	Main	47.0	4/28/82	SPTCo
San Francisco	Main	6.1	4/29/86	WP
San Fran/Santa Clara	Main		9/17/92	CAL-TRAIN
San Joaquin	Woodbridge	0.5	12/18/83	SPTCo
San Joaquin	Kentucky House	39.3	12/9/94	SPTCo
San Joaquin	Tracy	1.9	9/16/83	WP
San Joaquin	Manteca	6.6	5/9/89	TS

County	Branch	Mileage	Date	Railroad
San Mateo	Ravenwood Drill	1.3	6/22/87	SPTCo
San Mateo	San Bruno	2.5	3/31/94	SPTCo
Santa Clara	Lick	3.7	6/6/80	SPTCo
Santa Clara	Elm-Santa Clara	1.5	11/23/94	SPTCo
Shasta	Matheson	4.4	8/12/80	SPTCo
Shasta	Matheson	4.6	8/12/85	SPTCo
Siskiyou	Main	8.9	11/6/87	Yreka Western
Solano/Yolo	Holland	9.6	3/11/85	SN
Solano/Yolo	Holland	9.6	3/11/85	WP
Solano	Vacaville	4.2	3/29/85	SN
Solano	Vacaville	4.2	3/29/85	WP
Solano	Winter	8.4	6/21/85	SPTCo
Solano	Dozier	1.2	9/19/86	SN
Solano	Dozier	0.6	10/22/87	UP
Solano/Yolo	Dozier/Montzuma	11.8	11/30/87	UP
Solano	Dozier/Montzuma	22.2	7/2/93	UP
Sonoma	Main	2.4	8/4/80	P&SR
Sonoma	Main	10.7	6/17/84	P&SR
Sonoma	Sonoma	3.9	7/11/86	NWP
Sonoma	Main	0.7	12/19/89	NWP
Stanislaus	Riverbank		12/20/76	Amtrack
Stanislaus/Toulumne	Main	60.0	3/25/81	SilverFt
Stanislaus/Toulumne	Main		4/15/81	Sierra
Stanislaus	Turlock	2.7		TS
Stansilaus/SanJoaquin	Oakdale	27.6	9/17/84	SPTCo
Sutter	Rio Linda	6.2	4/8/85	SN
Sutter	Rio Linda	6.2	4/8/85	WP
Sutter	Yuba	3.8	7/1/85	SPTCo
Sutter	Tarke	3.3	8/2/85	SN
Sutter	Tarke	3.3	8/2/85	WP
Sutter/Butte	Chico	48.2	10/22/85	SN
Sutter/Butte	Chico	48.2	10/22/85	WP
Sutter	Yuba City	7.1	5/10/94	UP
Tulare	Main	0.6	5/20/83	VE
Tulare	Alpaugh	5.5		AT&SF
Tuolumne	Main	1.0	1/2/85	Sierra
Ventura/Los Angeles	Santa Paula	17.0	6/16/83	SPTCo
Yolo	Main	6.2	10/15/80	SN
Yolo	Holland	84.3	10/29/90	SN

ABOUT THE AUTHOR

Fred Wert is an active leader in the development of rail-trails. His early efforts included work with the Rails-to-Trails Conservancy where he served as its very first state chapter director, working in Washington State. Subsequently, he wrote *Washington's Rail-trails*, published by the Mountaineers Books. He works as a consultant to citizens' groups and public agencies on the development of rail-trails and is the Chairperson of the Pacific Regional Trails Council, an international organization promoting all types of trails and trail networking.

Mr. Wert is an accomplished cyclist and mountain climber and has been exploring railroad grades for ten years. He has visited more than 150 existing and future rail-trails, prepared a plan for rail-trails in Washington State, and promoted the 440 mile long Washington Cross State Trail. He is also the planning director for the Trans-Continental Trails Association, an organization working to develop a rail-trail across the U.S. and Canada.

INFINITY PRESS

Infinity Press is a small publishing firm located in Seattle, Washington. It specializes in guide books for the outdoors. A recent title which may be of interest is *Bakeries by Bicycle, A Guide to Puget Sound's Best Bakeries*, also by Fred Wert. This bicycle guide sends you to 47 of the best bakeries in the Puget Sound area via 27 scenic routes. If you would like to order a copy of this book, send $10.95 plus $1.50 postage and handling to Infinity Press, P.O. Box 17883, Seattle, WA 98107-1883. (Washington State residents please add $.90 sales tax.) If you would like an additional copy of *Rail-Trail Guide to California*, send $12.95 plus $1.50 postage and handling to the same address. (Washington State residents please add $1.06 sales tax.)

INFORMATION PLEASE!

We have done extensive research on the existing and potentail rail-trails in California, but it is difficult to keep up to date with all of the changes. We would appreciate your assistance in keeping revisions of this book current. If you know of significant changes in existing rail-trails, new rail-trails, or plans for new rail-trails, please let us know by sending information to:

Fred Wert
c/o Infinity Press
P.O. Box 17883
Seattle, WA 98107-1883

This is an opportunity to share information on your local projects with a much larger audience. We plan to include more complete information on future rail-trails in our next revision of this book. Thank you for your assistance.

Fred Wert